TWO THEORIES
OF MORALITY

TWO THEORIES
OF MORALITY

BY

STUART HAMPSHIRE

Warden of Wadham College, Oxford
Fellow of the Academy

THANK-OFFERING TO
BRITAIN FUND LECTURES
1976

PUBLISHED FOR THE BRITISH ACADEMY
BY OXFORD UNIVERSITY PRESS
1977

Oxford University Press, Walton Street, Oxford OX2 6DP

OXFORD LONDON GLASGOW NEW YORK
TORONTO MELBOURNE WELLINGTON CAPE TOWN
IBADAN NAIROBI DAR ES SALAAM LUSAKA ADDIS ABABA
KUALA LUMPUR SINGAPORE JAKARTA HONG KONG TOKYO
DELHI BOMBAY CALCUTTA MADRAS KARACHI

ISBN 0 19 725975 8

*Printed in Great Britain
at the University Press, Oxford
by Vivian Ridler
Printer to the University*

PREFACE

I AM very grateful to the Committee of the Thank-Offering to Britain Fund and to the British Academy for inviting me to give the Thank-Offering to Britain Fund lectures in 1976. This book is an expanded version of the lectures I delivered. I chose a topic which I hoped might fulfil the implied intention of the benefaction: that the lectures should be of some general interest outside a particular area of scholarship. I am grateful for the encouragement to compare in a summary way the two moral theories, Aristotle's and Spinoza's, which seem to me to have the greatest claim on their merits to the attention of a contemporary audience.

I also thank the Guggenheim Foundation for the support of a Fellowship during a period of leave from Princeton in 1968. Some work on the philosophy of mind at that time led me to reconsider the relevance of Spinoza's Ethics to some present issues in philosophy; and I thank Princeton University for its invitation to me to discuss some of the issues raised in this book in Gauss Seminars at Princeton in 1974.

TWO THEORIES OF MORALITY

1

A R I S T O T L E and Spinoza's moral philosophies, which are theories of practical reasoning and of human improvement, seem to me the most credible and the most worth developing of all moral theories in the light of modern knowledge and of contemporary philosophy. But they give very different accounts both of practical reason and of the improvement of human life at which practical reason should aim. They are competitors, and one cannot easily think of one theory as complementary to the other; rather one has finally to choose between them. The principal point of divergence between them is their opposing view of the relation between moral theory and ordinary, established moral opinions. Aristotle states clearly that moral theory must be in accord with established opinions and must explain these opinions as specifications of more general principles. An unphilosophical man of experience, who is of good character, usually reasons correctly on practical matters. Therefore Aristotle argues that acceptable moral theory will give a firm foundation to the principles that normally guide the decisions of the men whom we normally admire. Acceptable theory will not undermine established moral opinions nor bring about a systematic moral conversion.

By contrast, Spinoza in the Ethics claims to be showing the path to a necessary moral conversion which philosophical and moral theory introduce. As physical theory reveals a new world of particles in motion behind the ordinarily perceived world of medium-sized objects, so psychology and the philosophy of mind reveal a new psychic reality behind the ordinarily perceived passions and behind our ordinary purposes. Admittedly, most of our ordinary moral opinions are reaffirmed after the conversion; but a few of them are wholly repudiated, as depending on a false theory of the mind and on a false metaphysics. Those which are reaffirmed are supported by entirely different reasons; and practical reasoning is entirely reformed after the philosophical enlightenment. Therefore one can speak of two models of morality, which are opposed in their views both of the methods of ethics and of the prospects of human improvement; and I have always found a decision between them, though necessary, also very difficult and very far from obvious.

2

It is now possible both to think and to write about morality without epistemological and logical barriers being placed between the original subject-matter of ethics—'How ought we to live?'—and the reader who wants some direct or indirect answer to this question. The barriers have now been taken away, or have just gradually melted away; the barriers from epistemology and from the philosophy of logic and from the philosophy of language; the shibboleths of empiricist philosophy which represented the 'language' of ethics as a special subject of study. In 1949 I argued against that Humean theory of knowledge which obstructed discussion of morality in an article, 'Fallacies in Moral Philosophy', which was essentially a defence of Aristotle's methods in ethics.[1] The barriers in the theory of knowledge, which came from Hume and Russell, were at that time complicated, at least in Britain, by a fascination, first,

[1] See Note, p. 96.

with the single modal word 'ought', and, secondly, with G. E. Moore's famous argument about the word 'good' in *Principia Ethica*.

Few philosophers now subscribe to a theory of belief which excludes the possibility of there being beliefs about good and bad, right and wrong, which have respectable and intelligible grounds no less than beliefs of other familiar kinds. As for the word 'ought', the study of modal words shows that the word 'ought' has no particular connection with morality, but rather that practical reason of any kind involves the use of a whole panoply of modal words, of which 'must' and 'ought' are probably the most interesting. As for the word 'good', exhaustive inquiries into semantics and into practical reasoning have ensured that the word 'good' will no longer be segregated as belonging to some peculiar kind of discourse, or as indicating some peculiar speech-act. The thought that something is good, or the belief that it is, or the doubt whether it is, will be accepted as being normal thoughts, normal beliefs and normal doubts, whether in moral contexts or elsewhere.

The way is therefore open to looking for the underlying structure of one's own beliefs in the area marked by the word 'moral', without embarrassment about the logical form of the sentences in which such beliefs are typically expressed.

3

Two points arise about the phrase 'the underlying structure of one's moral beliefs'; this structure is something that one may look for and yet may fail to find, not only because one is not ingenious enough to find it, but perhaps also because it may not be there to be found. It is always logically possible that one's beliefs, in this area as in others, are too unrelated to each other, and that they exhibit too little coherence, to be subsumed under any sufficiently small, even if complex, set of more general propositions. In this case there would be nothing that could properly be called an underlying structure of belief. Then one's moral beliefs would, at the least, be ill thought out, and at the worst would be incoherent, and in need of revision. Secondly, a person's moral beliefs could turn out to be highly complex, and not susceptible of being subsumed under any relatively short list of general principles of which they are instances; and yet they could still be said to have a structure, if some clear account could be given of why they are complex in one particular way, and if some pattern can be discerned in the relations between the elements. Reflection on moral intuitions may not result in a relatively simple theory which satisfactorily, if roughly, explains the intuitions as derivable from more general principles. Rather it may result in a theory which explains why no such simple theory is to be found, and why no such simple derivations are to be expected.

The second point touches the phrase 'one's moral beliefs' and its interpretation. I interpret this to mean my own intuitions and beliefs, after they have been corrected by reflection and in so far as I consider them not to be merely thoughtless reactions, and in so far as they have that degree of explicitness that justifies the use of the word 'belief'. It is not reasonable to assume a very great coincidence of moral belief between contemporaries who have different metaphysical and religious beliefs. There must be a divergence in some moral beliefs between contemporary and similarly educated Christians, Catholic or Evangelicals, and on the other side Marxists and atheists. Even if there is a large area of agreement in the reasoned moral opinions of such persons, there must be crucial, sharp disagreements of a very untrivial kind. Not only this: but within a single lifetime a man may pass through more than one large reversal of moral opinion, and be converted from one set of moral beliefs to another. It is usual for a man's moral beliefs to change, and even to change fundamentally, between adolescence and old age. A change in philosophical beliefs, either in the philosophy of mind or in the theory of knowledge, may well be a reason, or even the reason, for a moral conversion, and for a radical overhauling of his moral outlook. The normal situation is that a rational person hopes through reflection to clarify his own beliefs by finding in them a degree of coherence which had not been evident to him before he clarified them.

Perhaps the hidden coherence takes the form of a belief that his actions should have a constant tendency towards producing some identifiable consequence, not previously isolated in the subject's mind; or perhaps it takes the form of a very general principle of justice that makes an otherwise miscellaneous set of moral prohibitions into an intelligible set of instances. The subject then may understand for the first time why he thinks as he does on a variety of moral questions which had not been brought together in his mind before. The clarification of intuitions, and the discovery of connections between them, are likely to lead one to revise some moral opinions which have previously been uncriticized. As Aristotle argued, there is a two-way traffic by which intuitions are modified by reflection on the general principles that explain them, and the general principles are qualified by particular cases that do not fit and fall under them. Aristotle therefore claimed that there is a strong practical interest, a guide to action, in moral theory. For example, he who convinces himself that some form of utilitarianism is the theory that comes closest to his moral intuitions has, from then onwards, a more definite and well-demarcated target to aim at. If I have gradually convinced myself, as in fact

~~I have, that there is an irreducible plurality of moral necessities constituting first, an order of priority among~~ necessary dispositions, ~~and, secondly, a way of life that~~ is to be aimed at, I again have a more definite vision of what ~~my intuitions have been pointing to. And this has~~ practical effects in my thought about political and personal problems. One has only fifty or so years to think, and to act on one's conclusions, if like Aristotle one excludes the possibility of moral coherence in childhood.

4

Specific moral opinions—for example, that torture ought not to be used, or must never be used, in the interrogation of terrorists, even if it saves lives and prevents more suffering—are often called moral intuitions, when stress is being laid on the unreflective, unphilosophical character of the opinions; and this is a standard and correct use of the word 'intuitions'. Beliefs that can be called intuitions are far from being peculiar to morality, and there is nothing questionable or irrational in having beliefs which are intuitions and which one then seeks to clarify and explain, in the sense of 'explain' already indicated. Beliefs that are intuitions are the natural product of unanalysed experience working on a mind that is adapted to making discriminations of a kind which the organism regularly needs to make. Recognition of perceived objects as being of a certain size is the obvious case of belief or knowledge which is usually intuition, as is also recognition of persons and reidentification of many other types of individuals. When you ask a man why he believes that it was so-and-so's voice that he heard, and what makes him think that it was, the belief is not normally discredited, nor made to appear irrational, if it turns out that he has no clear idea of why he thought so, or why he now thinks so, or of how he discriminated: that is, if he has no clear idea of the mechanism of discrimination and identification, and of those perceptual clues which would be studied in the psychology of perception, and which have in fact been used by him. The belief is not discredited unless people in general are unsuccessful, except when they can adequately explain their beliefs in this sphere by reference to their explicitly formulated grounds.

There are vast areas of belief necessary to survival within which intuition is not discreditable, and in which the mind operates by a mechanism of causes and effects normally unknown to the thinking subject and not easily open to his inspection. If it were possible to count beliefs, one could say that most of one's beliefs about the environment are of this character, being unsupported by conscious reasoning and even unsupported by reasoning which, though not conscious, is later traceable by reflection. My mind has been set to respond to certain clues with appropriate expectations and with beliefs, usually true beliefs, about the nature of the objects before me. It is admittedly always an advantage for me to know how my beliefs are caused, because I thereby acquire the means of methodically making corrections on occasions when the available clues are liable to mislead me. If a man understands the mechanism, he knows how it might go wrong, and he can take precautions not to assent to the beliefs that he would naturally form in deceiving circumstances. But Nature has not left it entirely to us, as Hume might say, to form beliefs by the conscious exercise of powers of inference in the sphere of recognition of objects and of persons, at least in the normal cases. The abbreviated inferences, which we may call intuitions, happen without the subject being aware of the successive steps in the pre-conscious inference. Such pre-conscious inferences guide not only recognitions and discriminations but also actions and manipulations. The compressed reasoning, which is the core of every practical skill exercised regularly and rapidly, can occasionally be brought to the surface and spelt out, when we are asked why we made on the instant the choice that we did—the immediate choice: 'because I thought that the ball would bounce the other way.'

Aristotle explicitly makes the comparison between perceptual judgements, of the kind that constitute recognitions, and moral intuitions, that is, immediate, unreflective moral judgements of the form—'this ought not to be done' or 'this kind of thing cannot be done; it is impossible'. I am arguing that it is a valid comparison in at least one important respect: in the relation between the belief that p and knowing why one believes that p. An experienced and consistently reliable observer is often not skilful in making explicit, either for the benefit of himself or for the benefit of others, why he believes that p, or skilful at isolating the more general principle that explains his beliefs. It is an advantage, even from a practical standpoint, for the subject to know the answer to the question 'why?' when his intuitions are questioned; and it is an advantage, even from a practical standpoint, for a person to have the ability to state the more general principle, or principles, which explain why he comes to the conclusions that he does in fact reach intuitively, and by compressed and pre-conscious inference.

The ability to say why, and to explain his conclusion, is a distinct intellectual talent, which has the great advantage of making occasional sources of error and of confusion evident, or at least traceable. An explicit criterion is available which was not available before; this makes deliberate planning possible, and, as Aristotle puts it, gives one a target at which to aim. Without a formulation of explicit principles, which gives one something definite to aim at, one is groping towards the target in the dark and one can be more easily misled by muddled conceptions of the end in view. My reason for reaching a conclusion on a practical moral issue may turn out to be a bad reason as soon as it is exposed and made the object of reflection. The intuition turns out to be mere prejudice, and the explanation of my belief may turn out to be no kind of justification of it. Similarly, the games-player's reason for playing the stroke that he did may on reflection be exposed as a bad reason, and, independently, the stroke may be shown to be a mistake, the product of a bad habit. But in neither case does this count as a reason for distrusting intuitions as a general policy; there is reason to check habits of thought by reflection.

Rawls in *A Theory of Justice* accepts this part of the Aristotelian theory of moral theory, as I have so far described it. But he substitutes for perceptual recognition a man's knowledge of his language, and of the relation of this knowledge to an explicitly formulated grammar, as his preferred comparison with moral intuitions and moral theory. A man of linguistic experience will immediately recognize solecisms, and will be able to avoid them; but he may often be unable to specify the rule of grammar which explains why they are solecisms. This is an attractive comparison. But I think it is more apt to mislead than Aristotle's comparison of moral intuitions with perceptual judgements and with recognition of objects. Our linguistic intuitions are required, by the nature of language as a means of communication, to conform to the linguistic intuitions of others: agreement in intuition, or at least convergence towards agreement, are essential to the main purposes which languages serve. For the same reason the rules of grammar, and of correct usage generally, need to be standardized in order that speakers should be understood by each other. Moral judgements of the form 'It is

B

wrong to do so-and-so' are not essentially expressions of conventions in the sense that they require ratification by general agreement. There is no incoherence in the notion of a man who explicitly accepts the fact that his moral intuitions diverge widely from those of most members of the society in which he lives, and who acts accordingly. He explains perhaps that the general principles that explain and connect his various moral intuitions are greatly at variance with those accepted by his neighbours. Perhaps he has different metaphysical beliefs or a different philosophy of mind. Not only is this possible; it is a situation that has often occurred and that can always be expected to occur. But private rules of grammar applied in defiance of one's linguistic community would be self-defeating, given that fluent communication is prominent among one's purposes.

It may be objected that the Aristotelian analogy between perceptual intuitions and moral intuitions is imperfect and that it conceals important differences. It does. One expects a man's moral intuitions to be explained by a comparatively few general principles which constantly enter into the abbreviated inferences. One even expects the explanatory general principles to cohere in some kind of order or grouping so that, taken together, they constitute a morality which is intelligible as a whole: intelligible as constituting a consistent plan of life, or as presenting a realizable ideal of conduct, in a normal span of life and in a normal setting, or as singling out a few achievements as supremely desirable before all others. On the other hand, the principles that explain the formation of this or that perceptual belief are vastly diverse, and there is no requirement that they should form an intelligible whole. The analogy is helpful only in so far as it draws attention to one complex common feature of the two kinds of judgement and belief: that the judgements are often immediately made, normally without a conscious process of inference, and the complicated steps towards the conclusion may be reconstructed either through the subject's reflection or by experiment or by some combination of the two. Therefore one can say about moral intuitions that theory may lie behind them, and yet they may be made without conscious thought or argument, as if they were immediate identifications of persons or things. The theory may be contained in the habit of reasoning from certain grounds to certain conclusions and not in explicit assertions rehearsed and present to the mind.

The thought that enters into one's moral judgements may be elaborate thought, and yet be inaccessible to the subject. Consider a case: suppose that one is sure that one must make a rule against the use by the army and police of techniques of interrogation of terrorists that amount to mental torture, and *a fortiori* against physical torture, and that this rule must be enforced, whatever the costs. Sensory deprivation is one form of mental torture, or near torture. Suppose that one might save many lives by finding a bomb in a public place and that this method of interrogation by sensory deprivation would be effective. Why do I think that the utilitarian judgement would be wrong in this case? It is not an emotional reaction, I think, but a reasonable judgement. Can I have a reason without knowing what it is? I might say 'Yes, that is my reason', when it is suggested to me. If Aristotle was right about the analogy with perception, I can have a reason without immediately knowing what it is.

Certainly it is more than useful, it is even necessary, that I should discover what the reason is that makes me think that it would be wrong to employ near torture, sensory deprivation, in interrogation of terrorists, wrong when even this is virtually certain to avert more suffering than is involved in the near torture. Perhaps there is a reason which, when exposed, will no longer appear to me a sufficient reason, or even a good reason. To repeat: the advantage is with conscious thought and argument, which allows for reflection and for evaluation and for checking of the unseen mechanisms of thought and for open discussion of these mechanisms. I may recognize, as a matter of fact causal judgement, that so-and-so is the reason which has been influencing me; but at the same time I may recognize that it is a bad reason, and therefore my opinion changes on reflection.

5

The word 'theory' has different connotations in the phrase 'moral theory' and in 'scientific theory'. In both cases 'theory' stands for a set of propositions, comparatively general ones, which explain a much larger, sometimes heterogeneous range of accepted propositions that seem to be more unrelated to each other than they really are. I use the word 'propositions' widely here to include instructions and prohibitions and rules. But moral theory, like any practical theory and theory of action, does not purport to be accurate in the sense in which a scientific theory must be accurate if it is to be acceptable at all. A moral theory is not necessarily, or even usually, falsified by a clear and indisputable negative instance. It is sufficient, as Aristotle remarked, that the moral theory, and the set of more or less general propositions that compose it, should turn out to be acceptable for the most part and on the whole, in actual experience, political or private. Suppose that one takes a conventional grammar of the Latin (or French or English) language as being a theory of the speech habits of the speakers of the language: one will expect there to be exceptions, some listed and some not, to the general rules of grammar and of word order formulated in the theory. Some of the exceptions will be not only listed, but explained, and some will be left as mere anomalies. Knowing the grammar will help a native speaker of the language, who has learnt to speak the language without the grammar; the grammar will help him to decide what is correct in doubtful cases, and it will be a guide to correct speech. Concurrently, actual speech and writing, in which he follows his intuitions of correctness, will occasionally lead him to revise the grammar that he had accepted hitherto as correct. Some exceptions will lead him to reject a rule that he had previously considered correct as a rule of grammar. Other exceptions will simply stand as odd exceptions, which are compatible with the rule holding for the most part and on the whole; there is a circle of mutual correction between practice and normative theory.

This type of theory—or, if you prefer, theory in this sense of the word—obviously contains propositions which are different in their logical relations to each other from the propositions that constitute a scientific theory. But it is very far from being a deviant and exceptional type of theory, or from involving a deviant sense of the word 'theory'. The distinction between theory and practice is as pervasive and important an opposition as that between theory and observation, or between theory and fact. Every worthwhile game, craft, or art has its theory, which stands in opposition to its practice; and in most games, crafts, and arts the relation between theory and practice, and the relation between knowledge of theory and excellence in practice, are controversial matters, as they have been in moral philosophy from its known beginnings in Plato and Aristotle. Is the man of experience and knowledge of the world who also has good dispositions by nature, generally to be preferred, as a regular source of sound judgement, to the man who has reflected on moral theory and who has arrived at sound conclusions at an abstract and theoretical level? Analogous questions are asked about other practical theories, for example, in games and crafts. The closest analogy for ethics has often seemed to be the relation between theory and practice in the fine and applied arts, though this analogy is far from being perfect; and the relation itself obviously differs significantly in the various different arts. There is a requirement that moral theory should exhibit a degree of coherence and comparative clarity, while this kind of constraint is not generally imposed on the very various theories that are put into practice in the imaginative and free or liberal arts—in the arts of music, painting and poetry, for instance. Secondly, a moral theory makes claims to be exclusively valid and not to be considered as just one of a number of equally valid or possible theories. Aesthetic theories concerned with works of the imagination are not generally taken to be to the same extent exclusive and competitive with each other.

A maxim of skill in a game or art or craft, a maxim of prudence in politics, or in economic management or in legal practice or in medicine, may be correct and may be a maxim that ought to be kept in mind and applied, even though there are circumstances in which it would be right not to act in accordance with it. The maxim may be correct within the art, even though it will on some few occasions conflict in practice with others which are no less correct within the art. This possibility of conflict is essential to practical maxims. No specification of a practical maxim or rule will exhaust the unpredicted variety of circumstances in which action may be needed. As the combinations of potentially noticeable features of situations is not finally circumscribed in advance, so the possibilities of conflict between injunctions to act, which have their grounds in those features, cannot be circumscribed either.

6

So far I follow the Aristotelian model of moral theory without reservation. From here onwards I must admit that identifiable doctrines from the Nicomachean Ethics are being amended and very freely interpreted at some points. The elements of moral theory that I have distinguished elsewhere ('Morality and Pessimism' and 'Aristotelian Ethics: A Defense') and that need to be more fully analysed are: the conception of an imagined best way of life, together with a conception of the specific virtues that are essential in it, and of some order of priority among these virtues: priority, that is, in the desirability of these virtues, and in the weight that is given to them in the over-all assessment of a line of conduct or of a policy, and also in comment on the character of a person and on his actions. That is the first element, still Aristotelian. All moral theories, which we would consider seriously, imply, when they do not explicitly state, a more or less precise conception of what virtues a man must have if he is to be praised in an unqualified way as a human being, and imply also an order of priority among these virtues; and they either imply or state a rather definite conception of the best way of life, and of the several distinct dispositions and interests which this preferred and sought after way of life will satisfy. The conception of a way of life has to include some social ideal, more or less detailed, depending on the priority that is given to political activities and to social usefulness. It includes also habits of behaviour and manners, observances, rituals of behaviour, which are not so much direct expressions of explicit moral beliefs as expressions of unstated moral attitudes and which can often only be identified with difficulty. The term 'way of life' has to be vague if only because it represents not only explicit ideals of conduct, deliberately chosen, but also ideals which have not been made explicit, or formulated, and which may be expressions of not fully conscious preferences, feelings, and ambitions.

This three-tiered theoretical framework—injunctions, order of virtues, way of life—is to be defended and justified in the same way that all theories have to be defended and justified: that it systematizes, and thereby explains, the moral intuitions which I share with many other men less incompletely than any other theory does. Secondly, the theory can find a place within the framework, and it can therefore explain, other and conflicting theoretical frameworks which cannot in their turn find a place for it. Other theories of morality—Hume's theory, Kant's theory, utilitarian theory, for instance—can be expressed within this framework, as prescribing ways of life which give differing priorities to essential virtues and to differing powers of mind and habits of action. These rival and non-Aristotelian theories are naturally not best expressed in Aristotelian terms, because these terms will not exhibit the grounds, external to ethics and drawn from epistemology and logic, on which the rival theories rest. But their substantial moral content can be expressed in Aristotelian terms.

Proceeding from the most vague general elements of the moral framework theory to the more particular, one comes to the first element, to moral prohibitions, the injunctions and judgements that exclude types of action, or forms of conduct, which must not be performed or into which a man must not enter; and these judgements and injunctions may apply also to attitudes and ambitions which a man must not, or more weakly, ought not, to have. The notion of moral prohibition, of what must not be done, of barriers and of restraint of vice or defect, may be more weakly expressed, in accordance with the general use of these modal words, as that which ought not to be.

But it is a mistake, introduced by some post-Kantian moralists, to think of 'ought' as the primary, or even as a primary, constituent of moral injunctions and pro-hibitions. The strong moral prohibition is most naturally expressed as 'I must not' and the injunction as 'You must'. This is not only a feature of speech and of the public expression of the thought. It is also true that the thought which is naturally expressed as 'I must do this' is a different thought from that which is expressed as 'I ought to do this'. Some actions, and some omissions of action, are impossible, out of the question, and not to be further considered, and they are impossible from a moral point of view, as con-trasted, for example, with a legal impossibility.

Our moral intuitions, however acquired, present us with a large number of prohibitions of types of conduct, types of action that must not be performed, because they are wrong, morally repugnant, shocking, indefensible, in-human, vicious, disgraceful. Reflecting on these intuitions in a critical spirit, and constantly looking for some simple connection between them, I ultimately find that they are not instances of one, or instances of a very few, much more general prohibitions or injunctions. They are irreducibly plural, and they single out various types of serious wrong-doing and despised conduct which are to be avoided. They are various, irreducibly plural, for the same reasons that the virtues and vices are plural; namely, that the ways of life which men aspire to and admire and wish to enjoy are normally a balance between, and combination of, disparate elements; and this is so, partly because human beings are not so constructed that they have just one over-riding concern or end, one overriding interest, or even a few overriding desires and interests. They find themselves trying to reconcile, and to assign priorities to, widely different and diverging and changing concerns and interest, both within the single life of an individual, and within a single society. They find themselves divided in their admirations and in their goals and they attach value to activities and dispositions which they know are normally incompatible, or which cannot easily be combined, or which cannot, under presently existing circumstances, be combined at all; even if it may sometimes be true that under better circumstances, and perhaps theoretically attainable ones, the activities could be combined. They also admire, and pursue, virtues which could not be combined without abridgement in any possible world: for instance, literal honesty and the constructive gift of fantasy, spontaneity and scrupulous care, integrity and political skill in manœuvre. Serious moral problems typically take the form of balancing strict but conflicting requirements, which Plato dramatized in the *Republic* by representing the man educated to be just as educated to combine and balance gentleness and firmness. As there must be conflicts in society, so there must be conflicts in the soul, and it is the same virtue that strikes the right balance in situations of conflict.

The conflicts between different virtues—justice and kindness, loyalty and fairness, honesty and the will to please—are paralleled, inevitably, by conflicts between prohibitions. I find myself in a situation in which I cannot both obey the injunction 'You must always support your friend when he needs your support' and 'One cannot be biased where justice is in question'. I have to weigh the relative weight which ought to be given to these now conflicting moral claims in the particular circumstances in which they have presented themselves. But this weighing is not a process of which no account can be given. On the contrary the reasons for thinking that, in the particular circumstances of the case, one claim overrides the other can be spelt out; and these reasons follow a certain general pattern, a pattern that invokes a way of life, and, subordinate to this, invokes an order of priority among the virtues and interests recognized as constitutive of this way of life. He who is able to tell you why he subordinates one of these claims to the other will not avoid disclosing his ranking of different types of human performance as more or less to be sought after and admired, and therefore as better or worse. He has in mind an ordering of dispositions and interests, which is an ordering of virtues.

Moral ideas are naturally first introduced and learnt by a child as a set of imperatives, seeming to be irreducibly plural and with reasons that are more obscure and less evident than the simple imperatives themselves. Becoming adult certainly entails looking for the reasons that lie behind the accepted imperatives and it entails questioning their apparent disconnection. The search for connections may end in several different ways: among others in the recognition of an order of priority among competing virtues, and in the recognition of complexity in ideals; and therefore in a recognized need, often recurring, to strike a balance at all three levels; first between conflicting moral claims, which may be rights, duties, or obligations, and secondly, between conflicting virtues, and, thirdly, between conflicting elements in a complex way of life which is sought after.

A defence of irreducible plurality is needed of a more systematic and philosophical kind, if hedonists, utilitarians of all kinds, and ideal contract theorists are to be rationally challenged. The defence must not try to show that utilitarianism and hedonism are untenable first-order moral opinions because they are logically incoherent; this would be to try to prove too much. He who believes that the discriminating, and reasonably altruistic, pursuit of pleasure and prevention of suffering is the only way of life worth pursuing is not so far involved in a logical confusion. If he is confused at all, he is confused about his reasons for believing that certain specific practices are wrong: perhaps about why he hates injustice, or about why he would not commit the crime of murder in almost any circumstances, or about why he admires honesty and loyalty as much as he probably does. If he has been thoroughly tested by actual and imaginary examples, and he has successfully shown that the balance of pleasure over pain, or the prevention of suffering, or the maximum satisfaction of preferences, are in all cases the only relevant considerations for him, one would have to admit that his moral beliefs were so far coherent and not confused. The criticism of them would have to move to a different level. One line of reflection, which might be persuasive, would stress the actual variety of conflicting ends which we know that intelligent men have had in view at different times and in different places, and which he has left out of account: an appeal to his imagination of possibilities which he may have overlooked or failed to understand.

Perhaps the case for recognizing an irreducible plurality of occasionally conflicting moral claims can be made stronger by an *a priori* argument. The proposal of a single criterion of moral judgement, as by utilitarians, is also a simplification of the virtues; all the virtues must be directly or indirectly derived from the two central virtues of active benevolence and active beneficence. The disposition to be fair and just is to be shown to be praiseworthy, in so far as those who have this disposition are likely, because of the disposition, to be more than usually beneficent; and similarly for all the other virtues. Those who find themselves compelled, in a particular case, to choose between justice and kindness, or between respect for the freedom for the individual and concern for the safety of the individual, have a computational problem; will a preferable outcome, on the whole, flow from preserving the freedom of the individual in these circumstances than from protecting the individuals against death and misfortune? A murderous disposition is dreaded, not because of the act of murder which is threatened, but because of the unhappiness and suffering that are the threatened consequences of the murder.

Adopting the contrary and Aristotelian theory, one may stress the conflict between duties and between prohibitions of other kinds, when one is thinking of conduct as expressing the character and dispositions of a man; also when one is thinking of a set of actions as expressions of a man's purposes, interests, and sentiments, and when one is describing and evaluating them from this internal point of view. In the common vocabulary actions are sometimes classified and discriminated by their outcomes and effects, and sometimes by the desires and purposes which they manifest, and sometimes from both points of view. A moralist who singles out 'the nature and quality of the act', as opposed to its likely or actual consequences, is probably thinking of the difference between killing a man and murdering him, between murdering and assassinating, between killing and letting die, between theft and fraud, between terrorizing and torturing, between lying and misleading, and so on; and he is probably thinking of the conventional and institutional classification of actions, which may be distinguished as a third type of classification, alongside classification by consequences and classification by disposition manifested, even though these types are not always distinct and are often combined in a single-action description. There is, for example, the human institution, historically recognized, of the assassination of tyrants; and therefore the killing of Hitler by the July Conspirators, had it occurred, would have been described as assassination rather than as murder, in a context in which the rightness or wrongness of the act was in question. The question 'Is assassination ever justified?' is a different question from 'Is murder ever justified?'.

Turning back to the previous example of sensory deprivation as a means of interrogating prisoners who are terrorists, one may raise the same moral question in three distinguishable ways. First, are the effects of this treatment of prisoners, both immediate and remote effects, so bad as to outweigh the probable good effects, and therefore ought the practice to be prevented? Secondly, is this treatment of prisoners so cruel and callous as to be morally repugnant and therefore to be prevented? Thirdly, does sensory deprivation amount to a form of torture of prisoners and ought it therefore to be prevented because all torture ought to be prevented, in virtue of the nature and quality of the act, an act intrinsically repugnant and an outrage? Within the moral theory which I am defending, all of these three ways of approach to the same blunt question—'Ought the practice to be prevented?'—are legitimate ways of approaching the problem, and none of the three is exclusively correct or is always to be given priority over the others. Most actions are at once the bringing about of an effect, also the manifestation of the desires and purposes of the particular agent, and also must be labelled as being of a certain recognized and institutionalized kind. A single-criterion morality, such as classical utilitarianism, deliberately makes an abstraction from standard action-descriptions as morally irrelevant except as indicating consequences, and utilitarianism particularly disregards institutional descriptions, and also descriptions of actions in terms of the motives and of the feelings expressed.

The single criterion, proposed by utilitarians, for deciding between conflicting moral claims finally makes all choices into a choice between various ways of ensuring a single result. These different paths to a single destination are to be understood, and their differences justified, as suiting the needs and interests of persons and communities with different histories and therefore in different situations. The apparent diversity of goals and of moral concerns is to be explained either by superstition or, in rational, free-thinking men, by the different utilities to be attached to the same virtues in different circumstances. The choice that a man may seem to have to make at a moment of crisis and conflict is not, on reflection, to be counted as a choice between two irreducibly different ways of life so much as a calculation of the efficacy of the superficially different ways of life in producing the unavoidably pre-ferred result: not a choice between ultimately diverging paths, but between routes that converge finally.

These implications of the no-conflict, single-criterion moral theory may be accepted by the theory's reflective supporters without qualms. Perhaps the argument against the single criterion should then be pressed further and made more general. That there should be conflicting moral claims, which are not to be settled by appeal to a criterion that is always overriding and final, may be represented as a consequence of the nature of practical choice for a language-using, and vocabulary-choosing and vocabulary-creating, creature. Such a creature has the means to present to himself alternative futures, either in specific or in vague terms, extending over long or short periods of time. He has the means to hope for, or to dread, tomorrow, next month, next year, middle age, old age, his own weakness or his recovery from weakness. He unavoidably thinks about his immediate and middle-distance future and he has intentions in respect of them. He knows many things that he will be doing soon, and at some time, and he knows when he will be doing some of them very exactly. The terms in which he thinks of his future vary with his social position, his temperament and

interests, and his moral beliefs. He can choose for himself
the terms in which he will both present to himself, and
plan, his own probable future, and possible futures:
within certain limits, which are set by the vocabulary and
habits of thought which he inherited or which he has
learnt and adopted. A way of life, inherited or freely
adopted, or a combination of these two, causes a man to
think of selected aspects and features of his future, which
become focuses of his desire or aversion, and to be wholly
uninterested in features that are strongly marked in the
moral vocabulary attached to another way of life. The
future, as he envisages it and as he describes it to himself
in advance, thinking about it and discussing it with others,
does not have all the interesting features which the actual
future has, when it comes for two reasons. First, the
future which is present to a man's mind never exhausts
all the features that might without absurdity be mentioned
in moral claims and comments; the description is never
an ideally complete description. The second reason is that
the future always has a margin of uncertainty, of unknown
contingencies, which were not expected and not intended.
Expectations and intentions at any time purport to include
only a few of the features which will be features of the future;
more that is of moral interest will normally happen than
could be either expected to happen or intended to happen.
There is material for conflict of moral claims, for example,
in the unexpected and unintended bad features of situations
which had been envisaged as having predominantly good
features; this on the objective side. On the subjective side
there is material for conflict of moral claims in the
experience of moral aspirations and emotions which do
not converge on single objects, or single types of object;
and the divergences are brought to the surface by common
situations in which features judged good and bad are
combined; and the divergence is particularly evident when

the good and bad are combined unexpectedly, in a complex situation, which has many contrasting aspects.

The conflict of moral claims arises from these two sides, subjective and objective, taken together. But it can be suppressed by an act of will binding the future and by a resolution that, as a matter of policy, superficially conflicting moral claims are to be settled by appeal to a single criterion. This is a decision to override the experienced conflicts for reasons taken to be of overriding moral and philosophical weight; philosophical, because they probably rest on an idea of rationality and of scientific method and on a rejection of unmethodical intuitions. Probably a theory of knowledge is invoked as support, one that dismisses the claims that I have made for the respectability of intuitions in this area. The decision to adopt a single criterion—for example, the greatest happiness or the least suffering or the greatest satisfaction of preferences—is made by modern utilitarians with an awareness that normal intuitions suggest a plurality of criteria, if criteria are invoked at all. Henry Sidgwick had anticipated a set of objections to utilitarian philosophy based upon ordinary intuitions in 'The Method of Ethics'.

The variety of situations, and of morally relevant features of situations, is always unpredictable and uncontrollable, and therefore no rational man ought to be sure in advance of experience that his single criterion will not produce unacceptable results. This argument has force principally for someone who accepts the Aristotelian epistemology of moral judgement; namely, that intuitions of the rightness or wrongness of particular actions in particular situations are the principal, though not the sole, grounds upon which general aims and long-term policies rest, even though there is a reciprocal grounding of judgements of right and wrong in particular cases in considerations about general aims and long-term policies. The famous

C

sentences on method in Book I of the Nicomachean Ethics say that thought on practical questions, whether prudential or moral, likewise in arts, crafts, skills, proceeds in an up-and-down way, from particular cases to general principles and back again from general principles to particular cases. But it must be admitted that there is no irresistible transcendental deduction which will prove that all practical thought must follow this pattern, if it is to be coherent. The utilitarian can argue that practical thinking in moral contexts is distinguished from practical thinking of all other kinds precisely by the single goal and by the simple criterion of right action, which are not to be found either in aesthetic contexts, or in any other kind of practical thinking. The man who claims to be sure that a single criterion must override all others for *a priori* reasons, in advance of all future experience, does not make an incoherent claim or an unintelligible one; nor does he commit himself to a policy which he cannot carry out in practice. A rebuttal, at once valid and persuasive, would need to suggest particular cases, actual and imaginable, which would illustrate the vast variety of possible situations of conflict between irreducible claims and goals, and which might cause him to doubt that his assurance of a single aim and simple policy coheres with his own thinking in particular cases. He may have failed to recognize the amount of forced simplification of difficult cases to which he is committed by the single criterion; and he may be deceived in his belief that no particular situation would ever disturb his *a priori* assurance about his overriding aim. He *may* be persuaded; but there is no absolute necessity that he should be, no final proof. Moral theory, like other practical theories, is not a matter for conclusive and irresistible demonstration. The superiority of one moral theory to another is established by showing that it gives a more simple and more comprehensive, and a less exception-ridden, account of the whole range of one's moral beliefs, and of the relation of one's moral beliefs to beliefs of other kinds, particularly philosophical beliefs. This is still the Aristotelian theory of moral theory. But perhaps one should now press the familiar modern questions about the objectivity of moral theory further than Aristotle did.

7

The checking of general moral theory against judgements about particular cases, and of judgements about particular cases against general moral theory, is a normal process of thought with which everyone is familiar. But there may be big differences in the emphasis placed upon the general as against the particular, and upon philosophical theory as against intuitions about particular cases. A Benthamite is gripped, like Bentham himself, by a philosophical theory that only one way of life is eligible by rational men who have got rid of those theological and moral superstitions, which suggest alternative ways of life other than the prudent pursuit of general welfare. He has philosophical beliefs about the requirements of rational methods of argument, and about the need to make moral issues determinate and clear, like the issues in an applied science. He probably believes, for instance, that the judgements which I have been calling intuitions are better assimilated to expressions of feelings and of emotional attitudes, which are natural in childhood and in pre-reflective societies, but which must be discarded by adults capable of systematic and scientific thought. The true utilitarian has the sense of unmasking and of penetrating behind pretences and superstitions and illusions to a single inborn and clear end of action which they conceal. He thinks that the superficially various virtues and various ends of actions are to be explained by reference either to utility or to surviving superstition, without remainder. If he is consistent in his utilitarian beliefs, and if he adjusts his particular judgements to his theory and acts accordingly, then he makes wrong judgements on occasion and in consequence acts wrongly: so I believe. Is this a mere confrontation between us without rational solution, or can the argument be pressed further? The suggestion that moral beliefs are not properly called beliefs is associated with the philosophical theory that very general differences of moral outlook are not accessible to further rational argument, beyond the stages of argument already mentioned.

8

The argument that might be pressed further is a philosophical one because it turns upon the relation of theory to practice quite generally. If the features of successive situations confronting us, which are relevant to our aims and interests, cannot be exhausted in our thought, and if we know this, then we are foreclosing, and restricting, thought if we cling to a single criterion of right action, and to one overriding aim, and if we exclude new considerations, and new features, from our attention. This will be true of every form of practice, whether it is a game, an applied art or craft, and the display and application of any kind of skill. There will always be a gap between the theory of good performance, necessarily stated in rather general terms, and the various details of actual good performances. The single criterion makes new, exploratory thinking on aims and ambitions redundant and unprofitable. Both new interests in the minds of persons, and new features of situations confronting them, have been given no place in their thought about their conduct and way of life. The exclusion is not only of newly existing and newly discovered, but of newly noticed and discriminated, features. But the development of a vocabulary, and of ways of imagining, which are apt for the making of morally significant discriminations, is an enterprise that does not come to an end and that is thought to be itself praiseworthy, and that is part of the interest of being alive.

In 'Thought and Action' I stressed the inexhaustibility of features that may be discriminated within situations requiring action and that may be morally interesting, and of the confinement within a morality left to itself, not to be further developed imaginatively, as a giving up of much of practical thinking. There is some force of rational persuasion, and there is more than rhetorical force, in an argument from the curtailment of further thought and imagination, as an implied consequence of a policy, to the conclusion that that policy is wrong: at least in the sphere of morality, in a wide sense. Having the power to invent ways to think about differently characterized alternatives, and to weigh good and bad features of situations and of actions and of ways of life on several different scales, is one distinction of the species; it is one power that makes friends interesting to each other and that make the species interesting to itself, and that makes its future interesting. The single-criterion and single-aim theories discard the peculiar interest of the species, and the interest of its future, as perpetually open to unforeseen alternatives through continuous thought. The single criterion arrests development, both historical and personal, by endorsing a single interest as supreme. The indefinite multiplication of satisfactions is a lesser prospect than the open possibility of the invention of new and unforeseeable ways of life.

The argument is not a transcendental argument, in Kant's sense, and it does not lead to a claim that its

conclusion is a necessary one. But it is a properly philosophical argument from the phenomena of choice and of
desire under alternative descriptions: an argument from
the nature of intelligence in the species and also from the
nature of language.

The argument runs: if the single criterion in ethics is
accepted by someone, that person decides to restrict the
peculiar powers of his intelligence and of his imagination;
and he decides to try to set a final limit to the indefinite
development of moral intelligence when he prescribes the
single criterion to others. This is not a logically impossible
conclusion; but it is an unconvincing one. The desires
of human beings are desires for objectives represented in
their thought under noble or agreeable descriptions, and
men act under the pressure of these descriptions, seeing
their actions as manifesting desirable dispositions and as
being part of an admired, or loved, or sought after, way
of life. Some large part of the value of their lives, as they
see them and as their friends see them, resides in the
imaginative thought that in this way informs their actions.
A simplification of thought, and the possibility of clearly
calculated solutions to moral problems, are often mentioned as reasons for accepting single criterion theories,
and particularly these reasons are mentioned by utilitarians.
But it is difficult, because unnatural, to discard the complexity of the thought by which we represent our dispositions and actions to ourselves, looking for better
descriptions of them, and a better understanding of them;
it is also an impoverishment, and a loss of the interest of
experience and of attachment to the future. Utilitarian
thinking is a kind of moral Esperanto. It forbids one to
cross frontiers into a different country, to be a tourist or
to emigrate, in thought. If a single criterion were accepted,
the future becomes uninteresting—or at least less interesting, both for individuals, and for any particular society;

and the future of mankind as a whole becomes less open. For such reasons as these a conflict of claims, which is not to be settled by a single overriding criterion, seems to be a necessity in our nature, and not just a superficial characteristic of practical thought at present, which it obviously is, but an essential one, not to be eliminated.

9

Conflict of claims, which each seem binding, and which cannot both be satisfied in some individual case, has been most carefully studied in jurisprudence. The reasoning that balances contrary legal principles, contrary in the particular case, is a kind of exact reasoning, studied and refined for centuries. It exhibits the familiar, circular pattern of general principles being used to guide decision in particular complex cases, and particular cases being used to modify general principles and to suggest new ones. Secondly, legal reasoning recognizes the unpredictable variety of circumstances which leaves a margin of indeterminacy, an area for legal argument and for judicial discretion, when laws and legal principles are interpreted and applied. Imperfect fit between general principles and particular cases is assumed in the working of legal systems.

This resemblance between the practical reasoning of lawyers about the law and practical reasoning on matters of moral concern is imperfect. For instance, it is a normal requirement placed upon legal arguments, when a conflict of claims is being settled, that the principles and reasoning upon which the settlement has been decided should be clearly and fully stated; they must be available for reference and usable as precedents in subsequent arguments and decisions. This is a requirement of entire explicitness. There is no such requirement placed upon the settlement of conflicts of moral claims, not even when the conflicting moral claims are in the public domain and call for policy decisions. It is not necessary, although sometimes it may be useful, that a carefully drafted formula should be promulgated, when a significant moral decision is made, and that it should be available as a precedent. The continuity that links moral decisions, whether by a public body or by an individual, is a constant tendency to contribute towards a preferred way of life, with a constant order of priority among the human qualities sustained in that way of life. Even when moral argument centres upon principles and a conflict between them, the rational basis of the argument is rarely an appeal to precedent, and to the need to conform to precedents, but rather to the over-all priorities in a way of life, which usually is an ideal rather than an established fact.

It is another aspect of the difference between a moral, and a merely legal, argument around a conflict of claims that imagination will not be called for in legal argument as it often will be in moral contexts. Aristotle assimilates moral reasoning, and the balancing of conflicting principles in particular cases, to procedures in crafts and arts, and also in medicine, because there is the same necessity that rules, and the theory behind the activity also, should always be imprecise, rough and ragged at the edges, liable to exceptions, lacking in ἀκρίβεια, which means accuracy in the sense of 'finish', as when a statue is unfinished because not polished, left in the rough, or when a drawing is left as a sketch. A trained judgement, together with some flair and a natural feeling for the subject-matter, enables the best performers to use the theory and principles of the craft, whatever it may be, up to the point at which they have to balance contrary principles and to find the right move without the guidance of principle.

This Aristotelian theory, which is a kind of epistemology of action, seems to me valid within its limits; and it still has a useful application to ethics, in reminding one of how unexceptional moral judgements are, in spite of the suggestions of empiricist philosophers. 'You must not stress rubato passages in your playing: that is bad' and 'You must not invest all your money in one investment' are sentences which are grammatically, epistemologically, and logically, neither more nor less anomalous and exceptional than 'You must not allow your purely personal feelings to influence your verdict'. Nor are any of them anomalous and exceptional as utterances. Also there are good theoretical reasons in each case which could be quoted in their support. The principle stated for the piano serves an aesthetic ideal which in turn has an aesthetic theory behind it. Within the theory the vice of excessive rubato is an instance of a more general vice that corrupts music. The principle of divided risk is justified by the function of investment and is part of a modest theory of investment. The moral principle is justified as constitutive of the virtue of justice as fairness and of the ways of life of which fair verdicts are a part. Each injunction can be supported both by *a priori* arguments, and also by appeal to the experience and judgement of experienced practitioners. They may come into conflict, in exceptional circumstances, with other general principles which are equally well supported by theoretical arguments and by long experience of particular cases.

10

There are further reasons why practical reasoning on moral questions should occasionally lead to conflicts of principles, even apart from the conflicts that attend all practical reasoning, no matter what the subject-matter.

Conflict of principles is overdetermined. Aristotle implied that moral questions are questions of finding the right balance among human interests, and he implied that each of the virtues, justice included, could be exercised to the full within a single complete life, and that there need be no final incompatibility between them. He claimed that, taking a man's life as a whole, there is no necessary incompatibility between the central virtues, all of which can be manifested in a complete life: though, he would add, only with luck. A man needs to have luck on his side if he is to realize the various ends that together constitute a desirable life. Aristotle claimed that there is no feature of internal human nature which entails that some virtues can only be attained at the expense of others in the long run, and the long run is a complete life: practical wisdom, for example, at the expense of theoretical understanding, or justice at the expense of friendship. Because of misfortunes, a man may in fact have to choose between friendship and justice, or to compromise between them. He will not usually be guided in the decision by any formula or test or clear criterion. He will have to make a judgement and to strike a balance guided by a conception of how the best form of life, taking his life as a whole, is to be realized. Each course of action perhaps has an evil aspect to it, and would be a blot on the record, a lapse from the conception of life as it ideally should be, even if an unavoidable lapse. The occurrence of conflict in particular cases depends on the uncontrolled and largely unpredictable turn of events in the external world, and in this sense on chance.

Let us assume that the dispositions towards justice and friendship are present in a particular man in an equal degree; he has these virtues, and he wants to be fair in making a particular award; but he also wants to avoid suffering, and he knows that he cannot, in the particular

case, do both these things, because the man who deserves
to lose will suffer greatly and the man who will win will not
be greatly pleased, nor would he suffer much if he lost. This
happens not to be an occasion on which a satisfactory
compromise can be made or a comfortable balance struck.
I am assuming one has to lean towards one prohibition or
the other, taking into account all the circumstances. Perhaps a just and truthful verdict has to be given in this case,
in spite of the consequences. The balance may be struck, in
the normal turn of events, in a complete life, in which both
concerns, a concern for justice and also kindness, are liable
to have their run: liable to, because a complete life itself
depends on fortune and not on reason, and cannot be
guaranteed.

A just balance has to be struck between competing
concerns and desires, not all of which can at all times be
equally satisfied, as a just balance has to be struck between
competing interests in society. Justice is in Aristotelian
theory the central moral virtue, subordinated only to
practical intelligence itself. A just man has sound intuitions
and a trained feeling for avoiding partiality. This dependence
upon intuition, and on perception of the just balance, is
not a sufficient reason for classifying such judgements as
neither correct nor incorrect. They are at least as determinate as are the judgements that are made in the practice
of any art or craft or game of skill. The correct balance to
be struck between competing values is that which exists
in the complete life of the fully developed human being.
Sometimes a run of ill-luck may make it impossible to
achieve the right combination of activities. But the nearest
approximation that the particular circumstances allow
is the right solution from the moral point of view. Flair
is required, a sense of proportion, a capacity to hold in
mind the different considerations, and not to be caught
by outbursts of unconsidered emotion. David Ross's book

The Right and the Good, the original work of an Aristotelian scholar, was often dismissed in the thirties and later as innocent self-parody, because Ross expounded his theory of prima facie duties and obligations, and of their typical conflicts, with a temperate tone and a judiciousness thought inappropriate to moral dilemmas; and he used banal and trivial examples. I believe that the theory of prima facie duties and obligations can adequately explain the most agonizing moral dilemmas in public and personal life as well as calm decisions on matters of public policy. The contrast between the cloistered Aristotelian scholar, unaquainted with tragic situations and violent alternatives, and the existential moralist, who confronts impossible choices with a glowing authenticity, is facile and misleading. The difference is more one of style and of tone, than of logic and of substance, as can be seen if one takes the standard examples from post-war existentialist writing.

In an occupied country a young man has to decide whether to join the resistance movement and thereby to bring punishments upon his family, who ask him to remain with them and to protect them. He recognizes both the claim of patriotic duty and loyalty and also the claim of loyalty to his family and the obligation to them which he knows that he has. Whatever his own set of moral beliefs, and whatever moral theory he accepts, if he theorizes at all, he would recognize that there are two apparent claims upon him. His own moral beliefs will determine both how he represents this apparent conflict to himself, and also how he argues with himself about them, if he is uncertain and if he needs to think carefully about them.

The valid point which an existentialist philosopher can make against Ross is that the conflict between prima facie duties and obligations, and the conflict of loyalties, in the example given constitute a conflict between two ways of life, and not merely a conflict between claims within a single way of life. There are extreme situations, not rare in this century, in which the subject reasonably sees himself as confronted with a choice between two different ways of life, which cannot be combined into one; and this great choice may be concentrated, and usually is concentrated, in a particular conflict of duties on a particular occasion, and it may never come up for consideration in an abstract way and as a general issue.

The notion of commitment has its place here. The young man is required to choose between the commitment to a life, or to a considerable part of a life, as a resister, as a member of a revolutionary movement, and as the servant of an overriding political cause, and on the other side the commitment to a life of decent usefulness and of family loyalty. The first commitment will demand the virtues of courage above all, of dedication, selflessness, also of loyalty; it will also call for violence, skill in deceit, readiness to kill, and probably also false friendship and occasional injustice. The second will demand the virtues of friendship and affection, gentleness, justice, loyalty, and honesty; it will also call for acquiescence in public injustice, some passivity in the face of the suffering of others, some lowering of generous enterprise and energy because of political repression. These are two different ways of life, because they demand different dispositions and habits of mind, different social settings, and different ends of action. The young man has to choose between two possible types of person, each with his own set of virtues and defects, now incompatible sets. He could set himself to become either of the two, as far as circumstances, his present character, and good fortune allow, but not both; and he may set himself to minimize the defects and to cultivate the virtues of his chosen way of life. But he has to establish an order of priority among his purposes, and among the dispositions that he will try to develop, before he can decide how to act in the particular situation of conflict.

That conflicts of duties sometimes pose great choices of ways of life, as well as conflicts within a preferred way of life, is a valid objection to Ross, and perhaps to most moral philosophies described as intuitionist. Intuitionists usually argue from the assumptions that the prima facie duties themselves are not only immediately evident, but also are evident for reasons that cannot be further explained and expanded; and, secondly, that moral conflicts have to be settled without appeal to any further considerations external to the acknowledged duties themselves. Both assumptions are contrary to experience, and they go a long way to explain the usual hostility to intuitionism as a moral theory and to explain its implausibility. The theory employed the word 'intuition' to mark a full stop to reasoning, where there need be no full stop. We know that the specific moral claims, in conflict in a particular situation, often uncover also a conflict between two ways of life, both of which incorporate sets of virtues greatly sought after and admired by the subject; but they are not compatible with each other, at least under present conditions and in this situation. The particular situation becomes exemplary and focuses the larger conflict. The choice between the two ways of life, with their constitutive virtues and defects, is open to reflection and to discussion: which virtues are incompatible with each other, under present and foreseeable social conditions and in the light of what is known of psychology and of ordinary human experience, past and present? Are the repugnant features, different in each way of life, ineliminable? Is a commitment to one of the two irreversible? Are both ways of life likely to endure indefinitely, or does one of them, at least, depend on social and political conditions that are temporary? These are just a few of the questions that are likely to be relevant. There would not be an undiscussable issue, not amenable to argument about matters of fact and to arguments about desirable alternatives, leaving the subject blankly staring at stark alternatives with nothing more to be said.

There are certainly conflicts of duties, and of other moral claims, such as obligations, which do not bring into focus a conflict between ways of life. Within a single ideal of character and action, and within a single conception of priorities among sought-after activities and interests, there must occasionally be an awkward impossibility of doing both of two equally necessary things; at least this must be so, if human interests, and the activities and traits of character and the sentiments to which men aspire, are not extremely simple, as utilitarians suggest that they are.

11

The idea of commitment to a way of life, and of the moment of choice between ways of life which are incompatible under present conditions, is reasonably taken as evidence against Aristotle's claim that there is a single, identifiable good for man, deducible from the nature of the species. Existentialists argue against Aristotelian essentialists that an individual's act of commitment to a particular way of life is the reality which is camouflaged by the pretence of a single way of life as the one good for man deducible from his essential nature. Does not the recognition of commitment, and of occasions of great choice, entail the denial that there is anything that can properly be called the good for man? Are there not in reality, and as experience teaches us, many different ways of life, which are reasonably counted as possible ideals to be aimed at? Does not history provide examples of the contrasting ideals?

At this famous crux distinctions need to be made, and they are distinctions that are not clearly made by Aristotle and by those who turned his philosophy into dogma. 'The good for man' can be taken to mean the set of activities, and corresponding dispositions, which after reflection are most sought after and which after reflection are most admired and praised, together with an order of priority among these essential virtues. So interpreted, the good for man can be made, and should be made, the subject both of *a priori* argument and of *a posteriori* argument from history and from personal experience. Which are the most admired, the most noble and praiseworthy and desirable, human characteristics and activities, after reasonable argument and reflection? The arguments are always imprecise and inconclusive; but still there is a convergence upon a list of generally recognized and familiar human virtues, which are differently ranked and stressed at different times and in different places. Put together in one definite order, they can constitute one ideal way of life, a distinct ideal of perfection and completeness, one among others.

At this abstract level, the good for man, the moral ideal, is to be compared with the ideally healthy man, the medical and physical ideal, a similarly abstract conception, not without its usefulness. Plainly men have greatly varied in weight and stature and dietary needs and muscular development and in resistance to disease at different times and in different places. Teaching medicine, a doctor might still show a diagram, and give an account, of a normally healthy man and of his functioning, perhaps tacitly pre-supposing that the normal man is to live in the climate in which the lecturer and his audience are placed and to be faced with similar conditions. The account would still be very abstract, until he complicated the picture by showing the effects of urban stresses, pollution, sophisticated diets, sedentary habits, and so on, together with the virtues of the body desirable under these conditions, which would not be so desirable for men living in South Sea islands, largely unclothed and with a plentiful local food supply, and a relaxed, but highly regular, way of life. Similarly, the good for man, the abstract ideal, will step by step be made more concrete, and be brought nearer to actual moral problems, as the social and political and cultural conditions in which a man or woman must design their way of life are more closely specified.

This analogy between the abstract moral ideal and the abstract medical ideal must not be pressed too far, because there is the obvious difference that health is one good thing among others, and its precise ranking among other good things may itself become a moral question, if there is a claim in some particular case that it should be sacrificed to something else that is valuable. There is a greater degree of freedom of choice, and a greater degree of indeterminateness, in arriving at the moral ideal than in arriving at the norm of good health, just because health is a subordinate end and an instrumental good and therefore it is open to a functional test; therefore with a subordinate good there is no place for the notion of commitment. The only value of the analogy is that it explains the distinction between 'the good for man' as the name of an entirely abstract ideal, and the limited moral ideals between which a man in fact has to choose, and to one of which he commits himself, in an actual historical situation. The good for man, in the singular, is not one of the ways of life, specifically described and related to specific known conditions, which an individual has to choose or reject in a particular emergency. Rather it is the vaguely described target which he ought to choose to aim at, in preference to a life of pleasure, another possible target, and in preference to making fame and reputation his aim,

D

and in preference to any other subordinate good taken from the set of good things which together constitute the good for man. It is useful for him to have a notion of the perfect human life, from which no considerable subordinate good is missing, even though he knows that he cannot attain it; and he knows that the constriction of his circumstances, and of his abilities and of his feelings and of his temperament, will always force him to make difficult decisions.

Within the good for man, the ethical ideal abstracted from all contingent circumstances, all the virtues are compatible: justice and the disposition to friendship, honesty and political responsibility, truthfulness and kindness. They are all part of the target, with some more central than others. The incompatibilities arise as soon as the contingencies of actual situations enter into the calculation, and the contingencies also of individuals' temperaments and abilities. It would be extraordinary good fortune if a man never had to choose between justice and friendship. When he does make the decision, in addition to the ideal he has a much more specific way of life in view, one that is attainable under the very definite limitations of his own social position and of his own skills and gifts and education. These limitations are not mentioned when the abstract ideal is constructed, an ideal valid for any man at any time and anywhere.

The essential virtues will form a coherent set of simultaneously realizable possibilities, if one at the same time imagines a society ideally adapted to protect and promote men's development and a population ideally adapted to the social roles imagined. Some of the potentialities, which are possible virtues, become incompatible with each other, and the moral ideal of perfection becomes unattainable, in tribes and cities and historical communities which force a choice between abandoning one virtue for the sake of another; and the perfect way of life is in any case un-attainable in any society that has a continuing history of conflict and bitterness.

The correct answer to the old question—'why should it be assumed, or be argued, that there is just one good for man, just one way of life that is best?'—is therefore an indirect one and it is not simple. One can coherently list all the ideally attainable virtues and achievements, and all the desirable features of a perfect human existence; and one might count this as prescribing the good for man, the perfect realization of all that is desirable. But the best selection from this whole that could with luck be achieved in a particular historical situation by a particular person will be the supreme end for him, the ideal at which he should aim. It is obvious that supreme ends of this kind are immensely various and always will be various. There can be no single supreme end in this particularized sense, as both social orders and human capabilities change.

12

Sometimes the name 'ethical relativism' has been given to the doctrine that judgements about vice and virtue, right and wrong, and about the ends of action, cannot be 'objective', because, first, they evidently vary as social conditions vary and vary over a wide range: also because there is no way of showing conclusively, or by probable and plausible argument, that one of the very different historical ideals is to be preferred to the other. The ethical relativist argues that there is no Archimedean point, external to a particular local moral ideal, from which all the local moral ideals can be judged and evaluated. To take these points in reverse: the Aristotelian denies that there is no external and neutral standpoint from which the various historically conditioned moralities can be judged. Precisely the force of the Aristotelian good for man is that it does single out, in necessarily vague terms, the perfect life for a man, taking account of his unconditioned powers of mind; and that this abstract ideal constitutes the permanent standard or norm to which the historically conditioned moralities can be referred, when they are to be rationally assessed. In fact the historically conditioned moralities do converge upon a common core and are not so diverse as the relativists claim. Courage, justice, friendship, the power of thought and the exercise of intelligence, self-control, are dispositions that in the abstract ideal are the essential Aristotelian virtues, although the concrete forms that they take greatly vary in the different socially conditioned moralities. The virtues of splendid aristocratic warriors are not the same as the virtues of a Christian monk; but they are not merely different. Each of the two ways of life demands courage, fairness or justice, loyalty, love and friendship, intelligence and skill, and self-control.

Every distinct way of life calls for these essential virtues, in one of their many versions and orders. They constitute the substance of morality, and the notion of virtue, and therefore of morality, are to be explained by reference to them. Relativism only becomes a plausible doctrine when it asserts that the particular forms which justice, courage, friendship, self-control, intelligence take will always greatly vary, as cultures and social structures vary, and that there is no strict order of argument which proceeds from an independently acceptable premiss to the conclusion that one of these embodiments of the essential virtues is to be preferred. As there is no Archimedean point of balance from which these embodiments, or concrete realizations, can be finally and conclusively judged in neutral terms, the fact that there is a rough convergence upon a common core of necessary virtues, abstractly conceived, is usually not relevant to practical decisions. It does establish that we can recognize different moralities as being all moralities, through the common core at an abstract level, just as we can recognize different codes of manners as all codes of manners, and different systems of law as all systems of law, in spite of the varieties of them.

To summarize: in many particular situations a balance has to be struck between the different virtues, and a balance has to be struck between the different interests and ambitions that are elements in the best current attainable way of life. This is not necessarily the kind of conflict which is intended when moral philosophers speak of tragic conflicts, irresoluble conflicts, and final conflicts; in the latter kinds of moral conflict the notion of striking a balance between conflicting virtues and conflicting duties, a balance that may prove to be the best one, when a whole life is considered, seems inappropriate. The difference between the two senses of conflict of duties and of virtues, or the two kinds of conflict, may be illustrated by the example mentioned above. The young man who has to choose between the resistance movement and the safety and happiness of his family does not have a choice, like that between generosity and prudence, which every normal man may expect to make from time to time, as one may expect to choose on occasion between justice and benevolence, or between fairness and friendship, or between truth and kindness; these may be called the normally unavoidable conflicts, requiring right judgement in the particular case and a balance between dispositions. The young man's conflict does not seem to involve finding the right balance between two elements of a single way of life; rather the choice can be seen as involving the abandonment of one way of life for another, although it need not be seen in this way.

Circumstances over which an individual has no control, however wise and far-seeing he may be, may destroy and make unrealizable a preferred way of life. Morality is in no sense autonomous and self-sufficient, as Kant wanted it to be, and choice is normally surrounded by uncertainties. As in a game or craft, or in medicine, the right choice often involves finding a way through undeserved misfortunes and hopeless accidents.

One may say that there is a conflict of values which is essential, or necessary, and not contingent: the conflict between aims, activities, and virtues, and consequently between prohibitions and injunctions, which have to be balanced in the right proportions, or, in the less appropriate terminology of welfare theory, traded against each other. At one level of achievement, the right balance between activities and dispositions in a complete life is precisely the good for man, the architectonic end. One can call the end for man a single criterion, if one is prepared to speak of a criterion which is designed not to yield determinate answers. Do you have a criterion by which you can distinguish good food from bad, if you learn that good food has the right balance between contrasting flavours, and when you ask what the right balance is, you are told that it is the balance which the really discriminating cook-gastronome perceives in the particular case? I do not intend by this comparison to belittle or mock Aristotle's single, overarching end. On the contrary, I think the notion of balance represents a deep moral idea. The combining in the right proportions of political and purely intellectual concerns, of reason and emotion, of public and private activities, of justice and friendship, of prudence and spontaneity, is a carefully thought out ideal and part of the Greek tradition, and was founded on the belief that the soul, and the body also, have to be a balance of elements. That is how they, and other living systems, work, and 'unbalanced', whether of mind or body, is one step away from 'destroyed'.

But other moral theories stress another kind of conflict, not admitting of resolution by intuitively judged balance: a conflict between two purposes or policies either of which, if chosen, would destroy any balance between essential, but competing, concerns and would involve a drastic amputation either way: this is the imagined existentialist case of the conflict between resistance to tyranny and loyalty to family in an extreme situation. As soon as one contrasts the two kinds of conflict, it becomes evident that the Aristotelian supreme end stands, as he intended that it should, on the border-line between being a meta-ethical claim and being a first-order moral idea. The notion of an overarching end, of a balance of virtues, may be rejected by a choice of a drastically specialized concern, or group of concerns, and therefore of an amputated existence, serving some entirely dominant interest; this has plainly been not only a romantic ideal, but a religious ideal also at various times. It seems to be the contrary of the Aristotelian good for man.

Can the argument between these apparent contraries be pressed any further? I shall argue that it can. Consider the romantic ideal of the man of imagination who, as an artist, neglects every duty and obligation which could stand in the way of the claims of his art upon him. He gives an absolute priority to the virtues of the imagination and to originality and to the invention of new forms of expression. If he is Flaubert, he will have reasons, the result of long reflection, rehearsed for his own thought and explained to his friends, repeatedly and throughout his life, for this ordering of the virtues of imagination and originality and for this preferred way of life. If he is Flaubert, he will not dispute the established and essential virtues of moral character; on the contrary he will insist that they are essential to any sustained achievement in art, as they are in politics and in private life. But he will adapt and correct and restrict the ethical ideal to take account of his historical situation, as he sees it, and of the peculiarities of his own temperament and emotional needs, as he believes them to be. He will find his justification in an argument that art has taken over some of the former functions of religion, and also that the distortions of modern life can only be rendered tolerable by aesthetic experience and the free exercise of imagination. He will argue also that the virtues of the family and of citizenship are beyond his reach, except at a very low level, and that his own power of thought takes the form of literary imagination, not of practical care for humanity, and also not of scientific intelligence, which he also deeply admires. He therefore derives the choice of his rather eccentric way of life, that of the dedicated and solitary artist, from the common core of moral ideals by an argument from the historical situation and the needs of his time, and not by an arbitrary choice.

He argues that his potentialities are not unrestricted by his inborn abilities and desires, and that, in the actual circumstances, he has to make a harsh choice and to discard some good things in order to realize others; a softer compromise would lead to an inferior achievement, with the abstract ideal still taken as the constant criterion of achievement.

That there should be an abstract ethical ideal, the good for men in general, is not inconsistent with there being great diversity in preferred ways of life, even among men living at the same place at the same time. The good for man, as the common starting-point, marks an area within which arguments leading to divergent conclusions about moral priorities can be conducted. The conclusions are widely divergent, because they are determined by different subsidiary premisses. Practical and theoretical reason, cleverness, intelligence and wisdom, justice, friendship, temperance in relation to passions, courage, a repugnance in the face of squalid or mean sentiments and actions; these are Aristotle's general and abstract terms, which do not by themselves distinguish a particular way of life, realizable in a particular historical situation. The forms that intelligence and friendship and love between persons, and that nobility of sentiment and motive, can take are at least as various as human cultures; and they are more various still, because within any one culture there will be varieties of individual temperament, providing distinct motives and priorities of interest, and also varieties of social groupings, restricting the choice of ways of life open to individuals.

In the light of this distinction between the abstract ideal, the good for man in a perfect life, and the relatively specific and limited way of life chosen by individuals at definite historical junctures, one may look again at the ancient question of the so-called objectivity of evaluations of ways of life, and of the virtues and the moral imperatives and the priorities which make up a way of life. The arguments around the abstract ideal, the perfection of men, are different in character from the arguments that lead a normally rational man to the choice of his particular way of life, or to his acceptance of the one that he finds himself born into and that he takes over without question. Arguments about the abstract ideal turn on the analysis of the notions of an end, on single or multiple criteria of rightness, on the notion of good, on the conflict of moral claims, and on what makes a context a moral one; in fact the arguments are those already deployed here. The arguments are largely philosophical and largely *a priori*, although they also mention very general features of common experience and of observed human nature.

The concept of morality, like the concepts of art or law

or custom or religion, defines an area of argument which has not greatly changed for two thousand years; the same central notions recur in analysing this concept itself and the nature of virtue and in discussions of the possibility that pleasure constitutes the sole good. But the arguments that enter into the actual decisions, the crucial ones, which determine, step by step, a man's way of life and his moral character, invoke the particularities of his historical situation, his temperament, his beliefs, particularly his political and religious beliefs, and his natural abilities and education.

Conclusions about the abstract ethical ideal, the perfect good for man, are to a high degree objective, though not in the sense that the argument for one abstract ideal can be conclusive and may amount to a final proof that this must be the ideal: but objective, in the sense that the validity and relevance of the supporting arguments do not vary with the varying circumstances in which they are invoked, but are universal and independent of any particular standpoint or assumed premises. Those utilitarians, who take pleasure to be the sole good and criterion of rightness, are committed to a set of implications which are as unavoidable today as they were when some of them were noted by Aristotle. There is very little looseness or freedom in the arguments in support of a single criterion propounded by the utilitarian and of multiple criteria propounded by the Aristotelian. The arguments converge upon a common pattern, and tend towards repetition, although it is always possible that new aspects of old arguments may be stressed, and even new arguments developed, by later philosophers.

On the other hand, the arguments that attach different priorities to different virtues, and that single out different moral imperatives as overriding, are uncontrollably various in varying historical situations and with the vastly varying circumstances in which individual agents may be placed.

Even the word 'virtue' itself now has an archaic and unnatural ring, sounding like a translation from Greek or Latin; and its more common use associates it with sexual abstinence rather than with a generally admirable character and achievement.

The facts and theories of society, and also the actual experience, on which moral arguments may draw, are not only vast, if one looks to history and to anthropology, but they are indefinitely open to the future. New forms of life are always to be expected, and the advance of knowledge and of technology continues, and new options are opened. No convergence is to be expected, and the more specific arguments cannot claim to lead to conclusions that are binding on all men at all times. This is the sense in which the arguments do not lead to judgements that can be called objective, while a judgement about the priorities among virtues in the perfect life can claim to be objective, even though it cannot be conclusively proved either by deduction or by experiment, nor by some combination of them. Hedonism is not a logically incoherent doctrine, if cautiously stated, but its wrongness is an objective wrongness, if, as I have argued, it is wrong. There is a sense in which the judgement that Shakespeare was a great writer is an objective judgement, even though it cannot be proved; it is objective in the sense that it claims, and receives, general agreement. There is also a sense in which a legal opinion—for example, the interpretation of a statute—may be objective, even though there is no proof of correctness, in the mathematical sense, and no experimental confirmation is to be expected.

In a difficult conflict of duties, in a case which amounts to a conflict between two ways of life, as when a man chooses between his obligation to his family and his duty to resist tyranny, the judgement of the right course will not be, and will not generally be taken to be, objective, in that sense. He who makes the decision, and commits himself to one moral priority, and to one principle, rather than to the other, is not necessarily making a decision, and entering into a commitment, which is either the wrong decision or alternatively fixes the priorities in an order which all men should observe at all times. The reasoning that supports his decision, if he reflects, will usually mention his character and his situation and the general circumstances of his time. Not only this: but he will probably recognize that his choice of a way of life is undetermined by the arguments that support his decision. In any difficult case of trying to choose the lesser of two evils, he will find himself 'weighing imponderables', and balancing considerations which do not tilt unmistakenly in one direction rather than another. He often would not wish to say that his decision on the right course is objectively right, in the sense that in making the decision he is at the same time claiming universal agreement for it. He has taken account of his own interests and abilities and limitations, and of his own situation and of his own past, and, in the light of these considerations, he has made his own commitment. His conclusion may be undetermined by the supporting arguments in the sense in which an unobvious judicial decision in a difficult case may be undetermined by the arguments; a contrary decision would have been arguable, not just plainly wrong. But the word 'commitment' carries a more positive implication; the implication is that he has himself recognized that his choice is undetermined by the reasons that support it, and, secondly, that he accepts responsibility for the choice as being his and his alone, without the support of any external authority.

The abstract ethical ideal, the perfect and most desirable life for a man in ideal circumstances, has to be mentioned only when a moral argument has been pushed to its limits and to its philosophical foundations. It is mentioned when ultimate priorities are in question. Otherwise serious decisions in moral contexts are typically decisions between imperfect alternatives, made in comparative ignorance of the outcome and of many features of the real situation, by a man who is aware that he must discard one essential feature of a praiseworthy existence in order to obey some even more essential imperative. Moral philosophy has sometimes unjustly been accused of banality and emptiness and unreality, because it remains at an abstract level, and because it does not reproduce the typical strain and difficulty of choosing between two courses of action, each of which seems utterly incompatible with the ethical ideal and a manifest evil, and yet the choice is in the circumstances an unavoidable one. There is the strain and difficulty of the necessary loss of an opportunity of happiness, or of justice, or of friendship, or of intellectual excitement, or of social reform, which has been chosen only to avoid a greater loss. This also belongs to the essence of morality.

I conclude that a man may understand and interpret his experience of moral problems, and of the serious difficulties that he has had in making important decisions, in Aristotelian terms; and that, if he does, he need not think that he has deformed the problems and lost sight of their real content, or that he has made them tidier and more definite and more rationally controllable than they in fact are.

It is a strength of Aristotle's moral theory that he thinks of morality and social policy as parts of a single subject, within which social policy is the more important and larger concern. A less often remarked strength is the thorough-going naturalism of his approach to moral problems in the Nicomachean Ethics.

He starts in Book I from biological concepts, and he

continues his argument with the use of them. The word ψυχή or soul marks the domain of biology, being the principle of life in living things. The vegetative part of the soul is no less a part of the soul than is the complex of human desires, and no less than the third and distinctive part, which is the complex capacity to think and to form designs for a whole life and for a complete way of life. The purposes proper to the species can only be attained in a complete life, and through the natural unfolding of the potentialities of the species, in the fitting social environment, and after the proper intellectual and emotional diet and training. Moral injunctions are to be thought of as a protection against a warped character, monstrous ambitions, corrupt appetites, and stunted and inhuman sentiments. They are to be thought of as a protection of innately preferred activities and sentiments, which bring pleasure with them, and against inhuman and conflict-laden activities and sentiments, which bring unhappiness with them. There is no independent, and no transcendental, sanction of moral restraints, and no authority external to men's experience of the workings of their own nature. The experience of ease and enjoyment of a way of life, as opposed to frustration and suffering, makes the crucial test, and men will in fact be guided by this test, if they are not governed by perverse passions. As felt pain warns us of some wound or infection in the body, so suffering warns us of some wound or corruption in thought or feeling.

By naturalism I here mean the habit of representing judgements about the moral strengths and defects of persons as resembling in most respects judgements about the physical strengths and defects of persons, and of representing virtue as an excellent state of the soul or mind, and vice as a diseased state of the soul or mind, manifested in action, just as health is an excellent state of the body.

But Aristotle has repelled many by the implication in his theory that there is a fixity in human nature, and therefore in the virtues, which justifies the complacent thought that the ends of action are immutable and fully known once and for all. This is the tidiness, and the limitedness, which have often been found both unrealistic and also morally repugnant.

I will not deny that the reflexive nature of thought, and the liberation that may come from it, and the accelerating growth of the physical sciences, do carry implications for moral theory which could not be recognized by Aristotle.

13

I have now filled in the reasons for the three stages of moral argument adumbrated in 'Morality and Pessimism': first, injunctions and prohibitions, then virtues and the priorities among them, and, thirdly, the way of life protected by these prohibitions and picked out by these virtues. On grounds of epistemology and logic I can still see no ground for apologizing for the defence of Aristotle. There is no comparably clear and comprehensive theory superior to his in the power to explain the range of our ordinary moral intuitions. But there is the barrier of modernity; by which I mean that there have been changes, both in knowledge and in ways of life, which have the effect of making Aristotle's reconstruction of moral, and particularly of political, thought seem incorrigibly incomplete. The succinct phrase for the barrier, and for the missing element, is the concept of freedom, which is applied both in individual psychology and in politics. It is notorious that this is the notion, imprecise and unmanageable, on which the barrier is built. Slavery was not for Aristotle an evil, even less the principal evil. The notions of freedom and of liberation are not to be found at the centre of Aristotle's ethics and philosophy of mind. There is no place here for the suggestion that supposedly free men are in a state of servitude, because of ignorance and thoughtless emotions, and that they need to be liberated through philosophical conversion, which will overturn many of their common-sense beliefs. The exercise of the crucial powers of mind, of real intelligence and good feeling, is not represented as a liberation from a natural state in which these faculties are blocked and not available. Nature and freedom are not in opposition. In a reasonably favourable social environment a character and moral temperament of the right kind will develop naturally by habituation. Similarly, his political thought does not have a place for freedom of individual choice as a value on the same level as justice in social arrangements; nor for respect for independence as a ground for action alongside respect for duties and obligations. His philosophy is, as it were, pre-lapsarian; neither in his philosophy of mind nor in his ethics is there some imagined redemption, or salvation, following upon a fallen state, a state of bondage.

A third aspect of the concept of freedom is missing, a third feature of a modern consciousness: the idea that all natural phenomena, including changes within the souls of men, are to be explained as instances of natural laws, and that nature is entirely uniform in the regular correlations of causes and effects: that there is a philosophical problem surrounding the idea of the morally responsible agent who has his own character to make and who is free to choose between good and evil; for it seems that his character directly, and his choices indirectly, must be the effects of innate and environmental conditions combined, and that he cannot be ultimately responsible for them, although he ought to be responsible for them.

The starting-point of ethics, as a philosophical inquiry,

is changed by the three-sided concept of freedom, and so also are first-order moral anxieties, both political and personal. The philosophy of ethics in modern times begins with some account of the relation between the scientific point of view and the moral point of view towards conduct and character. As this relation is explored, the difference between a man's knowledge of his own actions and purposes and his knowledge of other people's actions and purposes is investigated also. Spinoza stands at the barrier of modernity on the modern side, preoccupied with all three connected aspects of the concept of freedom— liberation from the passions, freedom in Society, and freedom in relation to the common order of nature, or, in short, metaphysical freedom.

14

When I first read Spinoza's *Ethics*, I was overwhelmed, as many others have been, by the fact that he was at once a moralist, writing from the moral point of view, and that he was also writing from the point of view of an imagined psychological and physical theory, deduced, as he thought, from first principles. He had not followed Aristotle in accepting the actual limits of human knowledge, as they were in his time. He made the assumption that no limit can be set to the development of systematic natural knowledge, and that a valid moral ideal must be compatible with the imagined future development of natural knowledge: more than compatible: that the enjoyment of such knowledge, and the desire to have the understanding that it brings, is a principal part of a reasonable man's ambition, and therefore of the moral ideal. Secondly, Spinoza considered the individual organism, which has to be both a receptacle of knowledge and an agent in pursuit of it, in

E

an entirely naturalistic way, without ascribing to a person any unexplained or supernatural powers, or any powers that are not to be understood as a complication of the powers of living creatures generally. Therefore moral enlightenment, and the improvement of men and of society, have to be the effects of understood and controlled causes in the natural order of things. In so far as radical improvement is attainable, it is attainable in much the same way that an improvement in men's physical condition may be attainable, by the application of a more systematic knowledge of causes: both of causes operating in society, as indicated in Spinoza's two political works, and also causes operating in the individual.

We are now in a rather better position to interpret Spinoza's account of personality, and of the mind–body relation, than previous generations have been, partly because we have machine models of the mind, or of some features of the mind, and partly because materialist conceptions of the mind are now advocated and disputed among philosophers with more care than ever before.

Spinoza's theory of the mind has at the least the following sources: first, the Epicurean tradition, which requires that the separable soul or spirit, subject of speculation and myth in the established religions, should be shown to be without function and non-existent. This tradition required that pleasure and peace of mind should be the goals of moral concern rather than a standard of perfection established by *a priori* argument. Secondly he rejected Descartes' theory of the soul as being like a pilot in a ship and argued that the person as a thinking being and the person as an extended thing must not be related externally, as in Descartes' theory; neither was merely an instrument in relation to the other, and neither had an absolute primacy. The difficulty and inconsistencies in Descartes' theory had shown Spinoza that the subject both of thought and of physical movements must be a person, and not in the one case a mind and in the other a body; and yet it is certainly true that thoughts can only be adequately explained by thoughts and motions by motions, as Descartes had argued. From Descartes also Spinoza takes the programme of reclaiming humanity from superstition and ignorance by a methodical correction of the intellect. But the method is different in Spinoza because there is no place for a mere resolution to accept only clear and distinct ideas, nor for sovereign acts of will. The improvement is to come through the recognition and constant awareness of the difference between clear and connected thought and mere confusion of mind, and from the natural and innate desire of a person to be as free and self-determining as he is able to be.

The third source of Spinoza's theory of the mind is the new scientific enlightenment of his time, particularly the new physics, and, more specifically, optics, with which he was closely concerned. I cannot prove from biographical sources that he had thought continuously about the physical basis of perception, and particularly of sight, and that this thought had been the inspiration that led to his theory of mind and to his theory of knowledge: and that he thought about the nature of light and studied perspective and the corrections that the eye and brain make to the inputs received. But I am convinced that I can infer this from the nature of the theory itself together with the few known facts of his life.

When an adult human being, a child still in infancy, and an intelligent animal perceive an approaching object, or a distant object, there is a physical input in each case and a physical interaction also. The physical effects are very similar in all three cases, different only in so far as the eye, nervous system, and brain are different; the animal's brain and optical equipment are different from the human ones, and apt to react to smaller ranges of differences of input. Like the adult, the infant and the animal react to the object with discrimination, and within limits intelligently, even though the thought that informs their behaviour is in neither case the conscious thought that is formulated in speech, or that could be so formulated. The motions in eye, nerves, and brain, in interaction with the environment, are to be explained within physics and without reference to any causes other than physical causes; and so also are the physical movements that constitute an element in the creature's behaviour. But the thought of the object seen as being of a certain kind, whether unconscious or conscious, unformulated or formulated, can only be explained by the thoughts that constitute reasons for further thoughts; and similarly also the thought that informs the behaviour is to be explained only by antecedent thoughts.

The thinking of adult human beings is of a complexity that allows thought about the causes that constitute reasons for their particular beliefs in a particular case. It allows also the further reflection on the goodness and badness of the reasons, as determined by an inborn standard of adequate thinking. So a man's perceptions, considered as thoughts, are indefinitely open to his corrections. The physical, bodily equivalent of this mental complexity is that complexity of the human brain which stores the effects of past inputs and which enables the new inputs to be combined with the traces of the old. Spinoza's speculation is that the material equivalent of the comparative autonomy of the rational, thinking man is the comparative independence of the physical structure which is the vehicle or instrument of thought, in the sense in which the eye is the vehicle or instrument of vision. The internal complexity of the human brain gives it a greater independence in relation to external influences. The traces of past inputs within the brain are linked and cross-linked in a vastly elaborate network; and this physical complexity is the material equivalent of the many-channelled capacity to learn and to acquire a variety of skills which distinguishes human thought from the less complex, and therefore more predictable, capacities of other animals. The human mind is relatively independent correspondingly. The thought that informs human behaviour and speech is not confined to routine reactions to the observed environment; it can proceed with some degree of autonomy, drawing on a vast store both of memory and of innate principles of reasoning.

The main subject-matter of morality is pleasure and pain, and the emotions, and the conversion of the emotions into forms of active and positive enjoyment. The emotions are thoughts about external things accompanied by affect; they are ways of perceiving reality with pleasure or suffering. A jealous man is a man with a belief about the causes of his suffering who traces the pain in his thought, whether conscious or unconscious thought, to a certain pattern of causes; he is therefore inclined to act against these causes. Just as a man corrects his first impulsive judgements of perception by reflecting on his limited evidence and point of view, so a man corrects his thoughts about the causes of his affects by reflecting on the inadequacy of these causal beliefs, and therefore on the inadequacy of his classifications of his own states of mind. Just as we come to realize that the systematic investigations of physics will reveal a different structure in the physical world from the structure of common-sense belief, derived from our perceptions of medium-sized objects: so a more systematic understanding of the connection of thoughts will show that our ordinary emotions, sentiments, and attitudes do not have the comparatively simple sources which we ordinarily suppose them to have.

15

There is one immense difference between ethics, which requires the correction of the intellect and the control of the passions, and medicine, the science that studies the strengthening of the body against disease. The correction of the intellect is an operation of thought upon itself. The instrument, and the material to which the instrument is applied, are of the same material. Doctors use physical agents as means to physical effects, and the laws of physics and of chemistry are necessary and sufficient to explain the physical changes that constitute a cure. The thought that informs the doctors' actions can be explained only by the thoughts, principally beliefs and desires, which the doctors have; and the relevant beliefs include beliefs about the laws of physics together with beliefs about the particular physical states of his patients or of himself, if he is his own patient. The moralist, correcting the mind and not the body, is a different type of agent, as is particularly evident when he is also his own patient, as he normally is. Then the thought of the need of a correction already amounts to a correction, or to the beginning of one. When a correcting thought is presented by a moralist to another person, as it were, to his patient, the thought, if understood, has an immediate effect on thinking of the hearer.

The conduct of men is governed by their emotions. Their emotions are constituted in part by their beliefs about the causes of their pains and pleasures. These thoughts about causes have their own causes in other thoughts, and all thoughts can be made the subject of other thoughts. If I think about the state of my body and of the causes of that state, or about your state of mind and its causes, there is no immediate change in the state of body, or in the state of mind, as an effect of the mere fact that I have thought about them. But my thought about the approaching object in my line of sight, and my jealous thoughts about my neighbour, are immediately changed if I start to reflect on my thinking that the approaching object is a so-and-so and on why I think this, and if I reflect on why I think jealously about the man. The original thoughts are changed, just because the new thought about reasons, even if it confirms the original thought, still adds new reasoning to it; now my reasons are more articulated than they originally were, and in this sense also they have changed.

To take an example from judgements of perception, which I believe were for Spinoza the crucial case, illustrating the thought–body relation: I think an approaching object is a hornet, and then I reflect on why I think this, and I decide that it is the size of the creature and its colour that make me think this and reasonably make me think this. Reflecting on the reason has confirmed the original thought; but the original thought has been added to and complicated by the further thought that the connection between reason and conclusion is for further reasons sustainable. The structure has become more elaborate. This argument ought not to rest on a principle of individuation for thoughts, as if thoughts were like pictures or 'lifeless images', which could be counted. Spinoza explicitly rejects this conception of thinking, which is to be represented as a more or less continuous activity, and not as a succession of distinct thoughts.

The thinking of a man with a knowledge of astronomy when he looks at the setting sun, and thinks of it as setting, is very different from the thinking of the simple peasant who sees the same thing and who in a sense makes the same judgement. The sun is associated in the astronomer's thought with an extensive theory and not with a few unsystematized pieces of knowledge of external objects. He understands, in the light of theory, his own tendency

to think of the sun as a comparatively small object suspended in the sky. He knows what makes him have this
idea and why it is inadequate. He still has the same vision
of the sun in the sky as the ignorant man. But this idea of
the sun is surrounded in his thinking with thoughts that
explain it, and, by explaining, correct it. Similarly, the
jealous man, who has acquired a deeper understanding
of his suffering, may find that jealous thoughts still occur
to him. But he will in his own thinking modify these
jealous thoughts with the fuller explanations that surround
them. The passions and negative emotions of men rest,
intellectually, upon an error of egocentricity and of short-
sightedness. One sees the universe as revolving around
oneself and one's own interests as central in it; and one
cannot see past the immediate environment to the vast
chain of causes that have led to the frustration of one's
own desires. Like the geocentric perceiver of the sun, one
ordinarily has a false perspective and a false scale, and
one's emotions betray this.

Spinoza's *Ethics* gives an account of a possible moral
conversion which takes the form of an intellectual
enlightenment acting on the emotions, which is not
unlike a religious conversion. The language of salvation
and beatitude that he uses enforces the analogy, a shaking
off of the burden of illusion and anxiety; there is an echo
of Lucretius. The enlightenment entails a change of standpoint and therefore a change of perspective; this is the
parallel with the correction of perceptual judgements.
A self-centred standpoint, determining a particular limited
point of view, is to be succeeded by an attempt to understand one's own beliefs, sentiments, and attitudes from a
more objective, less confined, point of view—ideally, from
the standpoint of impersonal reason: at the least from
a standpoint from which it is possible to examine the chain
of causes which led to the original beliefs, sentiments, and

attitudes. An observer of physical objects corrects his judgements to take account of his particular position in the world, of his angle of vision and of the effects of the imperfections and peculiarities of his own sense organs and of sense organs in general. The correction of the emotions is an analogous process of putting the painter of the picture into the picture, and of thereby making the original picture a feature of the scene alongside the objects that it depicts.

Scholars writing about Vermeer remark on this favourite theme of that time, particularly in Holland, of reflections within a picture; on the fascination with the refractions of light and with optics, with Leeuwenhoek's microscope, and with the grinding of lenses and with mirrors. Admittedly the picture of the painter, or the reflection of him, within the painting is a device of mannerist style, and one must not over-stress the analogy. But the parallel between correction for point of view in perception, and correction by understanding of causes of sentiments, is plainly there in Spinoza. He takes perceptual knowledge, and particularly the double involvement of mind and body in the acquisition of it, as the starting-point for his account of knowledge of all kinds and of thought of all kinds.

An emotion has an object, and is a way of perceiving the world painfully or agreeably. It is an interaction with external objects, as vision and touching are. But the interaction in the case of emotion entails not only pleasure and pain but also the desire to pursue or to avoid. Nothing prevents the emotional subject from stepping back to put his own jealous thoughts, with their accompanying pain, into their proper causal setting, except the strength of the passion, and the lack of reflection and knowledge of causes. The jealous thoughts are undermined by a wider, reflective view of causes; they are undermined in the sense that the subject no longer believes them. They may linger on as impressions, as my impression of the sun as a small object in the sky lingers when I no longer believe that this is its nature. The original and persisting thought may be described as bracketed, or cancelled, by being put into relation with a more comprehensive and coherent set of beliefs.

It is the characteristic of men's thought that it is reflexive and that the activity of thinking entails a process of stepping back, in order to attain greater objectivity, by making corrections for point of view. Active conscious thought in men naturally turns into self-consciousness, into thought about thought. This is the respect in which thoughtful creatures are, or may be, comparatively autonomous: comparatively, but in no absolute sense. Men act from the desires which their emotions engender, and which are constitutive elements of their emotions. Their passive emotions are the effects of external causes acting upon their drive to self-preservation and power through their conceptions, usually inadequate, of the external objects that are affecting them. Men will behave more reasonably, and the social order will be improved, if and only if at least a ruling minority of men are converted from egocentricity to detachment in their thought about themselves and about their relations to external things and persons. This conversion depends upon their realizing that their innate drive to increase their power and liberty requires disciplined thought, and an assertion of independence; this is a necessary but not a sufficient condition of the conversion. There may be emotional distractions that will stand in the way of clear and detached thought. Once a man realizes the power of thought, and exercises this power, he begins to enjoy the exercise and to feel the power of understanding, which is a positive pleasure, as men enjoy the exercise of physical powers. The drive for clear thinking and for understanding necessarily brings with it some self-knowledge and some degree of detachment from unconsidered and destructive passions; and this moral improvement cannot be achieved by any other means.

16

Spinoza's morality has as its terms of evaluation freedom of mind and independence, which are to be contrasted with confusion, obsession, and inner conflict. The ideal path of moral improvement leads from a state of being mentally confused, frustrated, and in a state of conflict to a state of being reasonable, clear-sighted, and at peace. The external manifestations of these states of mind will be hatred and conflict with other people on the one side and peaceful and friendly relations with other people on the other. The prohibitions and injunctions of conventional liberal morality, the prima facie duties, can be explained in two complementary ways; first, as being the prohibitions and injunctions that would naturally be respected by a liberated man, who would naturally want, for the sake of his own peace of mind, to behave as they prescribe and to follow the way of life which they protect. He would take pleasure in social harmony and friendship rather than in conflict and hatred. Secondly, the prohibitions and injunctions can be explained as the necessary protection of a social order that is indispensable to the free man's preferred way of life: reasonably peaceful and harmonious, reasonably tolerant, and free from either social conflict or tyranny.

Not all the conventionally accepted moral prohibitions and injunctions survive this double scheme of explanation. Some are only to be explained as consequences of superstitions and false philosophies, and cannot be explained as necessary protections of the way of life and of the social order which a free, intelligent man needs. Nor can they be explained as being principles of behaviour which an intelligent man will be naturally inclined to follow. They are therefore to be rejected. Most of them prescribe some form of asceticism, of renunciation of enjoyment without offsetting advantage, or they are tied to notions of sin and repentance, which in turn presuppose a personal God and divine Judge, which are illusions, projections of human passions.

Sustained pleasure is the mark of virtuous activity, together with attachment to a community of persons sharing an overriding interest in thought and knowledge. Hatred and aggression, manifestations of divided and fluctuating impulses, are marks of vice, because they lead to destruction and suffering and are incompatible with freedom of mind and with free inquiry and an interest in truth and in theory. Hatred causes an answering hatred; for Spinoza the principal problem of politics is the breaking of such reinforcing circles of hostility, which will always arise from the uncontrolled emotions of the mass of men who are still incapable of critical reflection.

One cannot stress too strongly that for Spinoza virtue is its own reward and that the word does not have its usual Christian association with renunciation of selfish interests in his thought. An admirable man, described in the last part of the *Ethics*, enjoys his own energy and the exercise of his powers of mind, and he steadfastly protects himself against the normal suffering of the world and against the loss of his independence. He participates in every effort to protect and extend freedom of thought, and his own happiness and way of life depend upon it.

17

Spinoza's doctrine makes morality, in the ordinary sense of the word a means to, and a by-product of, liberation from obsessions and from prejudice and an emotional enlightenment; and this doctrine entails a different relation between the philosophy of morality and morality itself: different, that is, from that which I have attributed to Aristotle. Let me use the phrase 'rational reconstruction' neutrally and say that both philosophers offer a rational reconstruction of the first-order moral judgements generally accepted within the social groups to which they belonged. Spinoza makes a clear separation between the reasons with which the conventional moralist explains his moral prohibitions and the reasons with which the philosopher would explain the same prohibitions. Asked why fairness is always necessary, and why the law is usually to be obeyed, and why incest is wrong, the philosophical moralist will look for an explanation within the double scheme already described: first, what the reasonably liberated man wants and needs, and, secondly, what arrangements are necessary to preserve that kind of social order and way of life which the man with an inquiring mind needs. Considerations of these two kinds will cause the philosophically enlightened man to accept most of the prohibitions of western liberal morality as reasonable, and will lead him also to cultivate most of the virtues which are ordinarily accounted virtues by just, peaceful, and tolerant men.

Spinoza does not anticipate Hegel's 'the cunning of reason' as a concept; but he certainly thought that the drive to self-preservation, and hence to a necessary modicum of social harmony, has led men by experience to respect the usual set of necessary prohibitions and to admire the usual set of necessary virtues. But men are also ordinarily myth-makers and imaginatively superstitious, and they have needed supernatural beliefs as props to moral restraint. The myth of God's judgements and God's punishments serve to sustain moral prohibitions which can also be explained as dictates of reason.

Spinoza's theory of personality entails a revision of moral theory which entails that the intuitions of the majority have no peculiar and final authority as they have in Aristotle's philosophy. Aristotle gives authority to moral intuitions because they are the unreasoned expressions of desires and needs implanted in essential human nature; it is the work of philosophical ethics to derive the intuitions from the various elements in the soul which explain them. Spinoza did not think of ordinary moral intuitions as expressions of a human essence; within his metaphysics there is no such thing. The rational justification of those intuitions which can be justified is found in their utility. They usefully prescribe, for the wrong reasons, the conduct which the free man wants generally followed for his own adequate reasons, which are quite different from the reasons of the unphilosophical man.

That every man pursues the extension of his own power and freedom to its furthest limit is not ordinarily recognized and acknowledged, although a reflective man may bring into consciousness this central drive for power and freedom. Rather the drive, or conatus, is postulated as part of a very general theory of individuality, which applies not only to men, but to creatures of all kinds; and the drive is particularly conspicuous in all living organisms. It is a natural necessity that our desires should be so organized that they tend to our own preservation, and to the extension of our power and freedom, as we conceive them, though this tendency will be disguised by the confusions of thought that normally inform our specific desires. The specific desires that move a particular man to action at a particular time are the effects of causes which operate in accordance with the discoverable laws of thought. The association of thoughts, the ways in which they combine to form sequences, are no less regular and intelligible processes than the processes of physical change in the body and brain. Spinoza held that it would be as much an offence against reason to question the law of causality in the psychological domain as in the physical; but the causality that links thoughts to thoughts has a different form from the causality that links one physical change to another. Conflict of mind and mental agitation are the normal conditions of men, and war and civil discord the normal external conditions of their lives. Although there are good reasons why it is so, and entirely adequate explanations of this condition, it is also true that it need not always be so. How is this possible? Is Spinoza's psycho-physical determinism compatible with the call for emotional conversion and liberation from conflict by an enlightened enjoyment of intelligence and freedom of mind?

The answer is to be found in the nature of thought: specifically in the reflexiveness of thought, in the capacity to form ideas of ideas of ideas indefinitely: in the intrinsic characteristic of thought to be self-correcting, when thinking reaches a first stage of complexity, as it does in adult men. The attainment of a degree of complexity in thought is inseparable from, and is an expression of, the same degree of complexity of associated physical structure; and this structure must be the brain. At a very low level of complexity physical processes in the creature are intelligible as functions of the inputs interacting with a more or less constant internal structure. The thoughts of the creature are thoughts that have as their objects these physical interactions. So a perception of an object is a thought of that object which has its cause not included in it; the cause is external to the thought. But when the percipient reviews and questions the perception, wondering whether it is to be endorsed as true, he is actively thinking; and the process of thought has its causes within itself and is not externally determined, or is not externally determined to the same degree.

The needed injunction therefore, the first commandment of a moralist, is the order actively to exercise the power of reflection, and to question immediate beliefs and sentiments. There should be a process of unmasking, of looking through the immediate classification of one's own attitudes and feelings to the more full, but disguised, connections of thought, which are the reality behind the appearances. That which a man believes about his own sentiments and desires in part determines what they actually are. So psychic appearances and the psychic reality are never to be entirely separated. No other appeal except the appeal to reflection is relevant; the passions, and the impulses which are part of them, are not to be controlled by the will, which is a fiction, but only by the self-altering activity of thought.

The power of thought and reflection exists in all sane men in different degrees, embodied in the complex structure of the brain. A man is free to change his moral opinions, and the emotions of which they are part, in so far as a change in them is not to be explained by a cause external to his own thinking, but is due principally to his own critical reflection, as far back as one can trace causes. The difference is one of degree, because no man's activity can be wholly independent of external causes. When a man sets himself the task of increasing his own freedom, he has set himself the task of directing and concentrating his own critical thinking, as opposed to reacting to external inputs. The activity of connected thought is the only activity of a person which may be autonomous and self-caused, in part and for limited periods. He thinks with his brain, as he sees with his eyes and hears with his ears, and the chain of his thinking may at any time be interrupted by an emotionally charged association of ideas, which is unconnected with the previous order of his thoughts. The power to think actively comes up against such limits continuously; but the power is always present in a sane and undamaged man. The power, which is freedom of mind, is nothing ghostly, spiritual, mysterious; it is a power which has its material equivalent in the vast complexity of the brain and of the brain's internal functioning.

The circuits of the brain function in accordance with the laws of physics, as do the sense organs and limbs and the human body as a whole. The ideas, which are ideas reflecting these bodily states, succeed each other in accordance with the laws of thought. The linkages are the linkages of ideas and these are regular and intelligible as sequences of thought, no less intelligible than the order of firing of neurons in the brain as a physical pattern. Spinoza notoriously claims that the order of causes is the same under the two attributes, in a sense of 'the same' which is not further explained, except in terms of the notions of substance and attribute. One can think of a physical configuration as conveying a thought and in another metaphor as being a vehicle for it. From the standpoint of the thinker, one can think of using one's brain, in the activity of thought, as one uses one's eye to see, or one's finger to feel. But one must not imply that a thought makes a physical configuration what it is, or that a physical configuration makes a thought what it is. Thoughts are only adequately explained by thoughts, and physical forces and configurations by physical forces and configurations. There are two utterly distinct, but indispensable, schemes of explanation with a common subject-matter, which is the total activities and reactions of human beings.

F

18

The freedom, which is the subject of Part IV of the *Ethics*, is the freedom that is conditional upon a degree of detachment both from the passions and from supernatural beliefs and fears: a familiar, Epicurean sense of freedom. But the background to it, the scientific determinism and the distinctive mind-body theory, lend the moral doctrine a new depth and weight of argument. From the standpoint of a rational, scientifically trained, detached observer, one can view all human beings in two ways: biologically and physically as organisms, whose movements and responses, described in the terms of physics, illustrate the laws of physics: secondly, and equally, as thinkers whose beliefs, questionings, desires, emotions, illustrate intelligible connections of thought. The standpoint of the solitary Cartesian thinking subject is that of a man questioning the reasonableness of his own thought and of the desires and emotions formed by his thought. He then appears to himself as a creature who is partly dependent on the action of causes external to himself, limiting his freedom of action: and partly as a thinking subject, who, surveying his desires, beliefs, and emotions and their causes, may rearrange them, and their interconnections, with some independence of the external causes which originally made them what they are.

As a Cartesian subject, he can step back from his moral beliefs and his desires which he sees to be in part determined, for instance, by social and family influences; and he can test their validity by reference to an inbuilt standard, which is his own tendency to rational coherence and consistency in thinking. The balance or see-saw between self-determination and external determination is the form in which moral experience presents itself: a swaying balance between consciousness of oneself as agent and as patient, a natural object, as a link in a chain of causes. This polarity is the real basis, correctly understood, of the distinction between virtue and vice, good and evil. Moral good and evil, as ordinarily recognized, are deduced from freedom of mind and slavery to the destructive passions. A political philosophy is similarly deduced from this metaphysical distinction. But you will object that the question still not answered is—how is the perception of a person, from the standpoint of an external, scientific observer, to be reconciled with that same person's perception of himself as partly self-determined, partly not? It seems that there must be a conflict between the two perceptions of the same object. The external, scientific observer sees an undivided illustration of effects following from causes and of natural law, while the subject, reflecting on himself, perceives an all-important discontinuity between his phases of active thought and his passive emotions and imaginations, externally determined.

This apparent conflict is not a contradiction. The phases and elements of active thought always have a beginning and an end, and are mixed with, and surrounded by, external causes that interrupt coherent thought and understanding. The conflict, which is not a contradiction, might be expressed in this way: from the standpoint of the individual the glimpses, and sudden experiences, of comparative freedom of mind and of clarity of understanding are the supremely important experiences, moments of pleasure, fulfilment, illumination. From the standpoint of a scientific observer the fact that the process of thought is sometimes, and to some degree, a self-contained one, rational in form, while usually it is not so, is less significant. The connections and linkages of ideas in non-rational, and in irrational, thinking are no less susceptible of explanation, and may be no less interesting to the observer, than the linkages that constitute a standard form of argument. An observer who is not merely curious and merely scientific in his interests, but who is judging and evaluating the person observed, will make other distinctions. He will be interested in the balance between self-determination in a man's thought and his mere responses to external causes, and in the degree to which a person is an active, rational thinker rather than someone who is governed by obsessions and by unchecked fantasies and irrational hatreds. An observer will need to make this kind of judgement if he wishes to change the beliefs or desires of the person observed. Spinoza remarks more than once in his two political works that one needs, for political purposes, to notice the difference between men who can be persuaded to be reasonable by argument and men who must be moved by less rational appeals to the imagination and to emotions.

Men normally recognize that most of their beliefs and desires were originally the outcome of causes outside their own thinking. But their thought takes the form of a review of their beliefs and desires; they have the means, in language, to ask why they believe and desire what they do. Moral philosophy reinforces this asking of 'Why?' and tries by its systematic arguments to make the reader more especially conscious of the standards of rationality which he is applying. Viewed from the standpoint of an observer, both his successes and failures, his periods of lucidity and his yielding to destructive passions, must have their explanation, even if the explanations are not known.

The contrast between the standpoint of the thinking subject, conscious of his own power to question his own desires, and the standpoint of the observer, seeking explanations of his changes of mind, is not to be found in Spinoza. Nor is the related contrast between the moralist, who prescribes and explains the best way of life and the virtues, and the scientist who discovers the causes that explain the actual virtues and vices of men in any particular case. This is a Kantian and post-Kantian contrast. I have added it as a gloss upon the notorious contrast within Spinoza's writing between the exhortation to correct the intellect and the simultaneous exhortation to abandon the dangerous superstitions that are associated with notions of free will. It is evident that for him these two exhortations are not only not in conflict with each other, but they are two connected, reinforcing parts of a single doctrine. Clearing one's mind of confusions and superstitious fears will always involve getting rid of the idea of oneself as an original cause and as a sovereign will and as an island in nature. The moments and phases of freedom of mind, which constitute a natural happiness, are moments when one is identified through one's own thought with the rational order of things. These are unegotistical moments, which bring satisfaction, excitement, and an elevation of mind, from two sources; first, the object of one's attention is intrinsically inspiring and sublime, and, secondly, one loses, in such phases of one's life, the sense of being narrowly confined within one's environment and of more or less helplessly reacting to it. There is a sense of power and of movement, and also of escape into the open and away from triviality, when one's thought moves into this larger natural element, which is the rational order of things, as revealed in physics and mathematics and in philosophy.

19

At this point I expect someone to press the following complaint: 'This may be a correct exposition of Spinoza, with some acknowledged modifications to fill a gap in his theory of knowledge: it is an exposition of a powerful and familiar set of moral attitudes, which contains a reverent, almost mystical, attitude to nature, and which traces cruelty and evil to their roots in inner conflict and which thinks of virtue as sanity and enjoyment of living and of vice as mental derangement. This is all very well', the objector continues, 'but what closely argued reasons can be given for accepting Spinoza's moral theory? Do you finally accept Spinoza's drastic reform of our moral intuitions rather than Aristotle's rational reconstruction of the reasoning that lies behind our standard moral intuitions?' I am inclined to think that Spinoza comes nearer to an acceptable position.

There are two principal reasons that influence me: the first is his theory of the mind and of personality, the so-called double aspect theory of personality, which insists that thoughts explain thoughts, and physical changes explain physical changes. The second reason is his consistent naturalism, and the theory of knowledge that goes with it. I shall consider them in order.

Spinoza's moral theory, which shows the path from mental servitude to enlightenment, is itself derived from the theory of the two attributes, thought and extension, under which a person's activities and states can be described and explained. This theory about the mind-body relation, and of how it must be understood by us, seems to me likely to prove correct, and my reasons for thinking this are independent of morality and of moral theory. If the double-aspect theory of the mind-body relation ought to be accepted, or at least is plausible, then some of our established ways of speaking about persons' abilities and powers and dispositions and emotions need to be reconsidered.

The double aspect theory of personality may be summarized as follows:

(a) As we see with our eyes, so we think with our brains, and eyes and brain pass from one state to another in accordance with the laws experimentally established in physics as laws of motion which are universally valid.

(b) All creatures think, and their behaviour can be described, both in physical terms, in terms of movement, and in mental terms, that is, in terms of what they want and of what they think about their environment. Human beings are exceptionally complex organisms, and are comparatively so much more self-determining and so much less determined by the immediate environment, that their desires and beliefs rise to the level of conscious desires and beliefs. Consciousness entails reflection and self-correction. It remains true that they can represent their behaviour to themselves as physical events and movements and also as the outcomes of desires and beliefs.

(c) Thoughts, including desires and beliefs, can only be adequately explained by connections natural to thought, as physical movements and changes can only be adequately explained as the effects of other physical movements and changes. The laws of thought and the laws that explain physical events are utterly different. We may observe, and rely on, correlations between physical changes and changes in belief and thought and, even more obviously, there are changes in our thoughts which are followed by physical changes. But there can be no systematic, theoretical understanding of these correlations, only an understanding of the mental sequences and the physical sequences separately and in their own terms.

(d) The natural laws that explain the movements of physical things, including human bodies, are those laws of physics that explain the behaviour of complex things by reference to the laws of motion governing their most simple elements. We can anticipate the logical outlines of acceptable physical theory, as it will gradually develop; but we are very far from knowing how the movements of very complex structures, studied by biologists, can be explained within the single physical theory, with its universal laws of motion. The human body is a supremely complex and sensitive physical structure, and Spinoza argues that we neither know nor can explain the powers which the human body possesses to act by itself, independently of intentions and conscious purposes. We do know *a priori* that all adequate explanation of reality, conceived as the domain of physical things, requires both universal laws of motion and a universal drive to self-maintenance in complex structures, which preserve their own nature while interacting with their environment. In the human body this drive to self-maintenance is appetite; and appetites in human beings are desires, when they are appetites of which we are, or can be, aware and which can be brought to consciousness.

We may intelligibly speak of a plant and of an animal as perceiving so-and-so and wanting so-and-so, in so far as in their interactions with their environment they are acted upon and react in accordance with their own nature. They receive information and they respond to the information received in accordance with their nature. We can therefore think of their behaviour and speak of them, in mental terms, as perceiving things and as having appetites. We can represent stimuli or inputs as perceptions, and the reactions traceable to their inner constitution and nature as appetites. In this sense we can think of all things, and not only human beings, as to a certain degree animated; this is the sense in which the plant registers the rays of the sun and wants water. These facts about the plant can also be expressed in purely physical terms as physical interactions, and must be so expressed, if we are looking for adequate explanations of their observed physical changes and movements.

Spinoza's point in writing of all things as in a manner animated is to assimilate human perception and human desires to universal natural processes of interaction with the environment, and thereby to undermine the Cartesian theory of an abrupt discontinuity between the workings of the human soul and the behaviour of other things in the natural order. The observed behaviour and movements of human beings can be described in terms of inputs and outputs of energy of various kinds, and the movements thereby shown to be instances of laws of physics, chemistry, and biology; with nothing said about the perceptions, desires, and intentions of the subject, or about the social and emotional significance of their behaviour. But we have to mention beliefs and desires, pleasure and pain, if we are to give adequate explanations of human behaviour as identified under descriptions that mark its social and emotional significance.

Appetite and perception, which become self-conscious as desires and beliefs in human beings, have a universal role in explaining the behaviour of objects in nature, and self-conscious desires and perceptions, which are one ordinary case of human desires and perceptions, may be regarded as a special case of interaction with the environment, from the perspective of a true philosophy.

(e) The linkages of cause and effect that explain thoughts are entirely different from the natural laws that explain physical changes. A thought is explained by being put into a sequence of thoughts which is by itself intelligible as connected thinking. Thinking is an activity, and we must not represent a sequence of thoughts as a sequence of discrete events, like a succession of images. Nor does the explanation of a thought consist in finding an experimentally established correlation between independently identified events. Rather it consists in finding the missing steps in a process of thought which is otherwise fragmentary and incoherent as thought and therefore unintelligible.

G

Spinoza implies that most of our thinking is not conscious thought, and claims that bringing to consciousness the cause of a desire or belief, by an effort of reflection, is the discipline needed in order to correct the passive emotions, which we do not originate.

(ƒ) There are two distinct orders of thinking, each of which are orders of intelligible thinking: the first is the order of the imagination, the second the order of the intellect. The first is governed by laws of the association of ideas, the second by the principles of logic. An adequate explanation of a man's particular desires, beliefs, and other propositional attitudes must refer them to one of these two orders, or to a combination of the two. In the order of the imagination a man's thoughts, and the emotions that are partly constituted by his thought, are determined by his perception of external things, and by his memories and associations. The capacity to trace and to criticize imaginative thinking is innate in men. If they perceive that the cause of, for example, their hatred of their neighbour is an ultimately unjustifiable belief about the harm that he has done to them, and if they perceive that this belief is due to an unrecognized association of ideas, their hatred of the particular man is suspended, or, as it were, bracketed. They perceive their own suffering differently, even if it continues, when they are converted to another view of its causes.

They have a more thoroughgoing and radical conversion when they abandon their more general belief, consciously or unconsciously held, that men are peculiar islands in nature, not subject to natural laws, and when they apply to the classification of their own feelings the theory of the emotions which a consistent and systematic philosophy requires. Such a philosophy shows that the men and women whom we believe to be the causes of our suffering are not uncaused causes, nor do they have free will; rather they are links in an interminable chain of causes. We perceive other people differently, and their relations to us differently, when we no longer isolate them in our minds from the natural processes of thought, and the natural processes of bodily change and movement, which they exemplify.

More important still: we perceive our own perceptions of the world around us differently, and hence we perceive our own emotions and judgements differently, when we see our own emotions and behaviour as natural responses in the common order of nature. When this happens, we are substituting the order of the intellect, with its laws of coherent thought, for the order of the imagination, with its laws of the association of ideas. One is replacing the false sense of transcendence, implied by Descartes, with a sense of being in the world, of *être au monde* in the phenomenologists' sense. One is replacing the sense that the world of objects is presented to the independent thinking observer, to an intelligence detached from the body, who sees the world from no particular point of view within the world. A true self-consciousness makes one aware that one is looking at, and responding to, persons and things from a particular place among other persons and things, a place defined by bodily existence, and with a mind that functions, both in perceiving and in guiding action, under the limitations imposed by this embodiment.

Spinoza in several places emphasizes the limitations of one man's, Peter's, knowledge of Paul, with the argument that Peter's thoughts about Paul must in the first place reflect more the changes in Peter's body, which constitute the physical aspect of his perceptions of Paul, rather than the true state of Paul. Thinking about his thinking, Peter can make the necessary corrections to his first thoughts, as he reflects on their sources and on his limited point of view.

If it is accepted that we have the two ways of thinking of reality, including ourselves—as a system of thinking things, and as a system of physical objects in space—the question about the equivalence of the two ways immediately arises, a famous crux in the interpretation of Spinoza. In one sense, or from one point of view, thought has a primacy: namely, from the point of view of the thinking subject, who reflects on his own thinking, and, following the order of the intellect, frees himself from attachment to his immediate environment. To have the power of conscious thought is to have the power of thinking about one's own thinking, in an indefinitely complex spiral of self-correction. From another point of view, that of the scientific observer looking for exact laws of nature, reality conceived as a system of physical things has a kind of primacy; because the world conceived as a physical system, in which human bodies are elements, is the first object of our exact inquiries and of our manipulations, under the important condition that our bodies are the instruments of our inquiries and of our manipulations.

The materialist is to claim that every mental state of a person, and particularly every emotion, can also be represented as a physical condition; and when a state of a person is represented as a physical state, it is represented as a state that can in principle be exactly controlled by the application to the particular case of the known laws of physics and chemistry. Reality conceived as a system of extended things is a domain in which exact and universal quantitative laws, experimentally testable, are to be found. The desire to control the mind-body state, and the knowledge of physical theory which exact control requires, plainly are themselves states of a person conceived as a thinking subject. A moralist and a philosopher try to change men's behaviour by producing thoughts about their thoughts, while a physician using thought, typically tries to change men's behaviour by changing their bodily states.

20

The essential and often neglected insight which follows from Spinoza's metaphysical doctrine of the two attributes, is that there is no incompatibility, and no competition, between the two systems of explanation, the immaterialist and the materialist systems of explanation. They are both valid and indispensable, and each is independent of the other and complete in itself. Therefore there is no need, and no proper place, for the kind of arguments which have divided both psychiatrists and the lay public when materialist conceptions of personality are proposed, and when physical cures are recommended for mental illness and for aberrant thoughts and emotions. The fantasies and unconscious wishes and memories of a mentally disturbed man have their own causes in his past perceptions and imaginations and emotions, and the causal connections between them follow the laws of thought. To cause the patient to become aware of the operations of his own imagination in engendering his beliefs and his wishes will cause him at the same time to understand his own behaviour as the expression of these beliefs and wishes. If this is achieved, and he understands the desires and purposes manifested in his conduct, these desires and purposes will be modified by his understanding, at least to some extent. His fantasies and imaginations are constituted by the concepts familiar to him, and are expressed in his language, and are linked to his memories. His conscious desires and beliefs, his conscious fears and his other propositional attitudes, bear the marks of his culture and vocabulary, and of the habits of thought which he has formed and of the unexamined, preconscious beliefs in which he was brought up. To explain one of his fantasies and imaginations, or of his more explicit and articulated desires and beliefs, is to situate it in a context of his thought and of his memories.

Sexuality provides the clearest untrivial illustration of Spinoza's theory. The sexual act may be described in terms of the various fantasies and desires that enter into the love-making; and these fantasies and desires will generally involve concepts, and an expressive vocabulary, which are culture-bound, and which are far from common to mankind. The sexual activity of an individual is imbued with his particular thought, his imagination, and his desire, and it reveals his individual mind with its weight of history. At the same time sexual activity is physical activity and its mechanisms are universally observable. We explain the sexual thoughts of the individual by supplying a wider context for them, which makes them intelligible as normal thought. The bodily processes we explain by the laws of physics and chemistry.

A man's passions may be so strong that he is unable to reflect and to substitute the order of the intellect for the order of the imagination in his thinking. Perhaps only a physical treatment of those bodily states which are the physical embodiment of his passions will change his conduct. His fear may be lessened by a chemical agent which acts on the physical state, which is the bodily aspect of his fear; then the intensity of affect is diminished rather as intensity of feeling is diminished by an anaesthetic or analgesic agent. There will be an adequate explanation within physiology of the chemical action on the nervous system and brain; but there is no intelligible and regular connection between the peculiar content of the thoughts that enter into his fears and the chemical transactions in his body. No very general correlation can be expected between an observed chemical transaction and the thoughts of men who have diverse languages, different conceptual schemes and memories, and different background knowledge; and such a correlation is in any case difficult to establish if a man's thoughts are not separately identifiable as discrete events, but only as steps in an activity of thought. The thoughts that enter into his fears, and that constitute beliefs and desires, have to be explained within the context of his imaginations and memories and other desires. When the full context is supplied, either the laws of association of ideas in the imagination or the laws of logic, or a combination of the two, will be discernible in the sequence of thought.

How a particular form of madness, or a particular form of neurosis, or any other aberrant state, is best treated in the present state of knowledge, is an empirical question, and cannot be profitably debated as an *a priori* issue. The *a priori* and philosophical claim, based on the double aspect theory, applies to the nature of adequate explanation; the theory prescribes what counts as a full theoretical understanding of thought, and what counts as a full theoretical understanding of physical and bodily states. There are evidently rough associations between some bodily changes, vaguely identified, and some changes in states of mind, vaguely identified. These are the rough associations which we learn by experience and on which we rely at a pre-theoretical level for practical purposes. But if experience suggests that my anger has caused my heart to race, the racing heart has to be explained as related to preceding bodily states by the laws of physics and chemistry, if a systematic, exact, and testable explanation is required. Singular caused judgements such as 'My anger has made my heart race' may be roughly true at their own level without being acceptable as possible parts of an adequate explanation. The judgement does not

allude to a natural law, and the association noticed is
not, and is not taken to be, an instance of one. It does not
allude to a theory applicable to the heart or to the passions.

21

Spinoza's variant of materialism, stated from the standpoint of the active subject rather than of the observer,
seems to me more than plausible, even though it is a
speculation that runs far ahead of any firm knowledge
in psychology which we possess. That explanation of
thought assumes an entirely different form from explanation in physics: that thinking is an activity not analysable
into discrete events, and that for this reason, among others,
explanation of thought must always be entirely different
from the explanation of physical processes: that our desires
and beliefs are changed by reflection on their causes, and
that to view our own emotions and desires with an
enlightened theory of mental causation in mind is already
to change these emotions and desires: that most of the
thought that forms our ordinary beliefs and desires follows
non-rational associations of ideas and is influenced by
unrecognized emotions and memories: that self-knowledge,
and the bringing to consciousness and to rational criticism
of unconscious thought, and of the emotions that are
formed by it, is the principal way to moral improvement:
that human knowledge is limited by physical factors, more
specifically, by the sense organs and the brain, and that
we can in our rational moments make allowance for
these limits: that human beings have not only the same
physical structures as other creatures, but also have
similar drives, as interpreted by biologists, and needs;
that their recognition of their subordinate position in the
vast natural order, and their emotional acceptance of this

subordination, is a central virtue that leads to the other virtues, and particularly to tolerance: that the virtues necessary to sustaining a liberal society naturally come from a philosophy which stresses the narrow limits of human knowledge, and which stresses the fact that most human behaviour is governed by unconscious memories and by hatreds due to prejudice, and that it is not to be governed by rational calculation. Therefore the self-righteous indignation, which is in accord with a belief in free will, has no place in liberal opinion of a philosophical kind, which will expect social improvement to come from a more detached understanding of the emotions and of non-rational thinking.

These doctrines are strengthened, and their direct relevance to morality reinforced, if the theory of evolution and of natural selection is added to the scientific background of Spinoza's naturalist ethics. With extraordinary insight Spinoza complicated the simple materialism of his contemporaries with his notion of self-maintenance of systems within systems and of the complex organization of different levels of living things. But his theory of knowledge, and therefore his moral theory, would have been more convincing if he had been able to represent the human brain and sense organs as having evolved gradually and as having conferred traceable advantages on the species, at least for a time, within the long evolutionary process. Secondly, the limits upon human knowledge, and powers of thought, no longer seem so certain and unalterable as they are within his theory, if accelerating additions to knowledge can be used to improve both the physical instrument of thought and thought itself.

22

Spinoza, like Aristotle, put public policy and political activity at the centre of morality. Unlike Aristotle, he explained both in his political works and in the *Ethics* the necessity of liberal institutions in an intelligent society. His principles prohibited bigotry and fanaticism, the denial of the right to dissent, hatred and aggressiveness in any form, repression and renunciation of life, and tyranny in any form; they prescribed the practical arts of political compromise, the defence of free thought, and the enjoyment of love and friendship and of active citizenship.

Spinoza substituted an emotional attachment to the natural order and its laws, and a curiosity about it, for similar emotions directed towards a transcendent Being. Corresponding to this abandonment of transcendence, and of the emotions associated with it, comes a changed attitude to human powers of thought and to the species generally. Human beings should think of their emotions and ambitions and conduct as being entirely natural extensions of the drives that animate all natural things. This thought should have a double effect: first, it should reduce the tendency to be wholly absorbed in local and temporary concerns, as opposed to permanent realities. Secondly, this thought of the whole natural order, to which human beings are subordinate, should evoke the same emotions of transcendence which are evoked by thoughts of a transcendent God in the Christian and Jewish religions. This double effect of the thought of the natural order, and of its power and permanence, is intended by Spinoza to replace the similar emotional effects and associations of the two dominant religions of the West, Christianity and Judaism.

He believed that a mystical, or quasi-mystical, intellectual love of nature as the Creator can replace mystical emotions before a transcendent God. The phrase 'Deus Sive Natura' makes this point precisely. I do not know whether this replacement is in general possible nor even how its possibility could be known. Personal experience and the evidence of literature suggest that, as the immanent source of what we see and of what we can imagine as an extension of what we see, including what we learn about its extent, order, and variety, nature can sustain those emotions associated with the superhuman. Therefore the dryness and thinness of a morality unsupported by the emotions that have as their object something transcendent seem to have a natural remedy: not exactly a nature mysticism, but certainly an exaltation and respect before the order and variety of nature. It is principally for this reason that the careless destruction of a harmless species of animal seems disgraceful, though this is not a sentiment of Spinoza's: not only because the destruction impairs natural variety, but, more important, because it expresses an ignorant attitude, and a false philosophy, of dominance, as if men were situated in the world as in their own garden.

These are vague ideas, associated with the word 'naturalism', and perhaps they are too vague for useful philosophical discussion. Certainly they need to be developed, and in a direction which is not anticipated in Spinoza's thought, which notoriously omits from its survey of the emotions, and of the activities of the mind, any account of aesthetic experience and of works of creative imagination. Kant's *Critique of Judgement* is here the necessary text, because it very plausibly analyses the pleasure and exaltation which may be felt in the face of nature, both as an order that is understood and as an order that can never be wholly understood. Secondly, Kant associates this feeling for nature both with enjoyment of beauty and with the enjoyment of art; and he sketches a relation between the enjoyment of art, and between the emotions that are linked with works of the imagination on the one side, and with morality on the other. More specifically, he argues that aesthetic enjoyment of works of art includes an enjoyment of imaginative genius, and that the characteristic of genius is that its products seem to be not artificial and not man-made, and not the effects of contrivance; rather they seem to be the effects of some natural force. On the other side, in the enjoyment of natural beauty, we have the impression of some natural scenes being adapted and formed to please our imagination, as if we were in a man-made garden, designed for our pleasure, and expressing human feeling. Therefore aesthetic enjoyment closes the gap between the artificial, which can be made by genius to seem natural, and the natural, which sometimes is adapted to the pleasure of human perception and imagination, as if it were artificial.

This is a nature mysticism, typical of the eighteenth century, which Kant had peculiarly strong reasons for stressing; for he had represented morality as the over-coming of natural impulse and natural sentiment, and as being in its essence reason's defiance of natural inclination and natural enjoyment. There is therefore an immense strain, the strain of a necessarily divided nature, between rational morality and natural inclination. For Kant aesthetic experience is indispensable as a mediation between the demands of reason and the demands of pleasure and inclination, and also between the need for order and coherence on the one side and for wildness and the creative extravagances of imagination on the other. For this theory of early romanticism, the landscape garden, or the cultivated ruin in the park, or the folly, are the images of an ideal relation between man and the rest of nature, from which he is otherwise alienated.

This romantic idea of the need to recapture naturalness, otherwise lost in the exercise of reason, comes near to explaining the metaphysical emotions which can take the place of those associated with transcendental religions; particularly Kant's theory of genius and of originality in the imagination as being the channel through which natural insights, otherwise lost, return to the human mind, as it were, unobserved and by unknown paths. We seem to ourselves to be brought into contact with a permanent natural order through works of imaginative art, whether literature, music, or painting; there occurs the familiar feeling that works of genius reveal an otherwise concealed or muffled reality, not accessible to science or to any conscious reflection.

It is a fact, evident in experience and in literature alike, that human concerns, even a concern with the future of the whole species, are apt to seem too small until they are brought into relation with some transcendent order; and this is partly because of the thought of the imminence of death for the individual, and also the thought of the ultimate extinction of the species. The claims of morality seem not easily reconciled with the idea of an individual's life, and the life of the species as a whole, as small episodes in a vast natural process, unless through an exercise of understanding the episode is given a special place within the natural process: and understanding here includes reason and the imagination also. Aristotle argued that in the exercise of theoretical reason in the pursuit of truth, human beings play the immortal as far as is possible for them, and are absorbed in permanent realities. He represents this activity as the summit of achievement, the highest virtue. Spinoza's suggested escape for transience is through natural knowledge and a mystical sense of the unity of nature, which will enable some men to have a vision of a permanent order and to identify themselves with it, at least through their inquiries. This certainly is one relief from transience, and an old and very well-known one; and there is no doubt that intellectual discovery and inquiry can be an escape from a sense of triviality and impermanence, at least for some men. But I think that for many men those emotional experiences which can be called aesthetic are also escapes from a sense of triviality and impermanence, and in this respect have some of the force attributed to mystical experiences. They suggest to the mind, while the experience lasts, not only an exaltation, but also the thought of being in contact with some permanent reality or pattern. This is a vague thought, but it is a familiar one both in experience and in literature. It is linked in my experience with those thoughts of separation from nature, and of recapture of naturalness, which are set out in philosophical terms by Kant. Reading the *Critique of Judgement* I recognize a set of thoughts and sentiments directly drawn from experience, but with one major qualification; Kant's philosophy still places human beings, as scientific inquirers and as moral agents, at the centre of the Universe in respect of the absolute value that attaches to them and to their interests, and that attaches to nothing else, except derivatively.

One may agree with Spinoza's suggestion that this humanism, reinforced by Christianity and by Judaism, ought in consistency to disappear with philosophical and scientific enlightenment, and particularly with a clear and non-Cartesian theory of personality and of thought.

A final observation: these two intellectually persuasive theories of morality, Aristotle's and Spinoza's, rest upon different visions of human life. Although Aristotle represents theoretical interest in eternal realities as the highest virtue, he still thinks of a single human life, taken as a whole, as constituting a good or a bad total performance, including the exercise of theoretical reason within the performance. He imparts a strong sense, to be expected in a biologist, of the limited and natural span of a life and of the completion of successful activity which may be achieved within that temporal span. One might say, in caricature, that the argument of the Nicomachean Ethics leads the reader to view a human life, and particularly his own, from the standpoint of his eventual obituarist.

Spinoza does not lead one to assess an individual's life as an outstanding performance, or as a poor performance, within its natural constraints, because he has a different idea of time and of our experience of it. It is not the total performance within an individual's life that counts, but the occasions of transcendence, when a person is able to understand things, including himself, *sub specie aeternitatis*, rather than *sub specie durationis*. Behind the ordinarily experienced temporal order and the temporal units, such as a human lifetime, there is an intellectual order with units that are the significant units within systematic theory; and a desire for understanding and enjoyment of this intellectual order should override all other interests. But arguments about temporal order, in its relation to intellectual order, are beyond the range of these lectures.

NOTE

Further reading directly relevant to these lectures includes:

'Fallacies in Moral Philosophy', by the present author, published in *Mind*, **58** (1949).

'Ethics: a Defence of Aristotle', by the present author, published in *University of Colorado Studies, Series in Philosophy*, No. 3 (1967).

Both these articles were reprinted in *Freedom of Mind and other Essays*, published by the Princeton University Press (1971).

Morality and Pessimism, by the present author. Leslie Stephen Lecture. Cambridge University Press (1972).

Freedom of the Individual, by the present author. Chatto and Windus (1975).

The Significance of Sense, by Roger Wertheimer. Cornell University Press (1972).

Moral Notions, by Julius Kovesi. Routledge (1967) (and in Paperback 1971).